D1617058

UPSTREAM MARKETING

UNLOCK GROWTH USING THE COMBINED PRINCIPLES OF INSIGHT + IDENTITY + INNOVATION

TIM KOELZER & KRISTIN KURTH

CO-FOUNDERS OF EQUIBRAND CONSULTING

GREENLEAF
BOOK GROUP PRESS

Published by Greenleaf Book Group Press
Austin, Texas
www.gbgpress.com

Distributed by Greenleaf Book Group

For ordering information or special discounts for bulk purchases, please contact Greenleaf Book Group at PO Box 91869, Austin, TX 78709, 512.891.6100.

Design and composition by Greenleaf Book Group
Cover design by Greenleaf Book Group and Mimi Bark

Publisher's Cataloging-in-Publication data is available.

Print ISBN: 978-1-62634-751-9

eBook ISBN: 978-1-62634-752-6

Part of the Tree Neutral® program, which offsets the number of trees consumed in the production and printing of this book by taking proactive steps, such as planting trees in direct proportion to the number of trees used: www.treeneutral.com

TreeNeutral

Printed in the United States of America on acid-free paper

21 22 23 24 25 26   10 9 8 7 6 5 4 3 2 1

First Edition

For Kit, Matthew, Madeline, and Isaac.

Contents

PREFACE

CONTENT MARKETING. INFLUENCER MARKETING. SEARCH marketing. Social media marketing. Inbound marketing. Outbound marketing. Re-marketing marketing.

These are all proven ways to promote your business, though they are *downstream* in nature. They're mainly tactical tools, delivered digitally, and designed to sell products already developed. While downstream marketing is necessary, it's not sufficient.

Winning marketers relentlessly focus on expanding their playing field using a strategic approach to identify and fulfill unmet customer needs. Creating and capturing new market spaces and building strong brands is the domain of upstream marketing, and the focus of this book.

We developed this book using upstream marketing and the three combined principles of insight, identity, and innovation.

We captured insight from hundreds of client executives and industry experts, including a deep dive on seven companies profiled in this book: Amazon, Apple, Google, Nike, Southwest, Starbucks, and The Walt Disney Company.

The book's identity—the *Upstream Marketing* title and cover design—was created to appeal to a distinct target audience: you.

Innovation concepts, including a minimum viable product, were used to create the book you're now holding in your hands or reading on a screen.

The same principles used to create this book are employed by EquiBrand Consulting every day to help grow strong brands and businesses for our clients.

EquiBrand, a strategic marketing consultancy, was founded over twenty years ago. The company name comes from two words—equity and brand. *Equi* ties to the economic and analytical side of marketing, making cash registers ring. *Brand* relates to identity and innovation, creating something out of nothing.

As classically trained marketers, we are functional specialists and work across a spectrum of companies—from global Fortune 500 companies to venture-backed startups, within business-to-business and business-to-consumer settings. Our client list reads like a who's who of top global brands and businesses, and projects where we've played a major role have contributed over $1 billion dollars in sales to their businesses.

To support our client work, our team conducts extensive research to identify and further develop best management practices. It's a continuous loop where we discover and apply these methods to client situations, then feed the learning back into our frameworks to transform businesses.

Everything we've learned about upstream marketing is summarized and explained here for the first time.

We hope *Upstream Marketing* provides you with the inspiration and tools to execute it within your organization.

As you read it, visit www.upstreammarketing.com to learn more and engage with us. Here, you'll find additional content—templates, training videos, and implementation services.

We're always interested in feedback that helps us review and refine our approach. So, as ideas come up, drop us a line, and let's get started!

CHAPTER 1

UPSTREAM MARKETING— AN OVERVIEW

"It is well known that 'problem avoidance' is an important part of problem-solving. Instead of solving the problem, you go *upstream* and alter the system so that the problem does not occur in the first place."

—Edward De Bono, author, *Serious Creativity*

"Because the purpose of business is to create a customer, the business enterprise has two—and only two—basic functions: *marketing* and *innovation*. Marketing and innovation produce results; all the rest are costs. Marketing is the distinguishing, unique function of the business."

—Peter F. Drucker, author, *The Practice of Management*

"As to methods, there may be a million and then some, but principles are few. The man who grasps *principles* can successfully select his own methods. The man who tries methods, ignoring principles, is sure to have trouble."

—Harrington Emerson, *management consultant and efficiency expert*

THERE'S AN OLD STORY ABOUT a man searching at night on his hands and knees under a streetlight, looking through the grass. A passerby stops and asks what he's looking for, and the man replies, "The keys to my car." Being helpful, the passerby joins in the search.

After some time, with no success, the passerby asks whether the man is certain he dropped the keys near the streetlight. "No," he replies. "I lost the keys somewhere across the street."

"Why look *here* then?" asks the surprised and slightly irritated helper.

The man responds, "The light is much better here."

If one thing is clear from our years of management consulting, it is this: Most organizations search for growth in all the wrong places. They believe an ad campaign, refreshed website, digital marketing funnel, more content, social media, sales promotion, or similar effort is going to drive sustainable growth.

Many CEOs, business leaders, and marketing managers see their playing field as largely fixed and overemphasize downstream marketing, failing to embrace the power of upstream marketing to build strong brands and transform their business. In some cases, they've surrendered the foundational principles of marketing to the digital era, including an overreliance on marketing push tactics.

The purpose of *Upstream Marketing* is to change that perspective and provide the principles, tools, and techniques to redefine the playing field and unlock growth.

This book introduces the concept of upstream marketing, defines it, and establishes a new framework to drive growth, drawing on core principles of insight, identity, and innovation. These principles, when combined with six upstream marketing best practices and four business framing questions, facilitate a strategic approach to fulfilling customer needs and creating new market spaces.

The principles and practices are universal and apply to any organization, regardless of industry, company size, or geography. So, whether you are an executive in an established company, a small business owner, on the board of a nonprofit organization, a student of marketing, or just interested in understanding the concept of upstream marketing, you can benefit from this discussion.

BEST PRACTICES IN CORPORATE GROWTH

"What's the headline?"

That's the question the lead partner asked our consulting team during an internal strategy session. It was the summer of 1997, and Tim was working for another consulting firm, before EquiBrand.

Our team was assisting a global apparel manufacturer develop a *process* to stay at the leading edge of innovation. The client wanted to define a standard approach to growth and innovation, then implement it across the half dozen or so business units within the company.

The project had two broad parts—a design phase and an implementation phase. The design phase kicked off with an internal assessment to get up to speed on our client's business and establish initial hypotheses. How were leading companies able to consistently grow their business more, and faster, while others in the same industry lagged? What were the major steps, activities, outputs, and requirements to achieve above-market growth?

Our job was to define best practices that distinguish "good" companies from "great" companies, then use that information to design the process. (If this "good to great" approach sounds familiar, that is because it's a fairly common way to benchmark best management practices.)

We selected six companies across a spectrum of industries based on financial performance and company access: First Union (now part of Wells Fargo), Gillette (now part of P&G), IBM, Nike, Gap, and The Walt Disney Company. In exchange for participation, the companies received a copy of the study findings.

With the list solidified, we divvied up the companies across the team and set out to gain best practice insight. The first profile company our sub-team visited was Nike. At the time, Michael Jordan and the Chicago Bulls were in the middle of their second three-peat world championship performance after their first three-peat win a couple of years earlier.

With Jordan back in the game and at peak performance, Nike's Air Jordan was generating huge revenues for the company. Nike had a significant athletic footwear business, though not much else. It may be hard to imagine now, but in 1997, there was no Nike Golf, no Nike Soccer, and no Nike Tennis.

Through research before the visit, we learned that one year earlier, in 1996, Nike had signed a then little-known, twenty-one-year-old Tiger Woods to a $40 million, five-year contract, despite Nike's limited presence in the golf category.

Also in 1996, Nike made clear its commitment to the world's most popular sport, soccer, by signing the CBF—the Brazilian Football Confederation, making good on CEO Phil Knight's belief that, "We will only truly understand football when we see the game through the eyes of Brazilians."[1]

Looking at the business through the eyes of the consumer was a recurring theme in assessing Nike. It became even more apparent during our visit to Portland, Oregon.

When our team pulled the rental car into Nike's headquarters, we thought we had made a wrong turn. We were expecting a collection of corporate office buildings. The Nike grounds, though, looked more like a college campus or sports complex. Soccer fields. Volleyball nets. Running tracks. It was early morning but felt like lunchtime or a Saturday afternoon. Employees were out on the fields, playing, working, and experiencing the category and brand.

Nike's culture, deeply associated with athletes, sports, and design, was vividly on display that day. Phil Knight's mantra was evident. His team looks at the business through the consumers' eyes. In fact, the Nike team *became* the consumer, gaining more in-depth insight while having fun!

We didn't get to meet Phil Knight that day, but did spend time with his lieutenants to understand Nike's approach to marketing and innovation. The interviews helped define how Nike successfully innovates product after product, time after time.

Weeks later, the full consulting team met to compare notes and debrief research findings across best practice companies. We had hoped to uncover a standard *innovation process* to replicate with our client team. That didn't happen. The companies were too different, and no single process emerged.

Instead we found a common set of *principles* across all best practice companies, which was far more impactful. We used case evidence and systematic review to "structure the unstructured" in preparing findings. Our team then presented initial recommendations on innovation best practices and obtained approval from the client to employ them in the pilot phase.

This second project phase was where the study differed from typical "good to great" comparisons. After the design phase, we worked directly with the client to pilot a new approach to innovation real-time with a couple of their divisions before refining and rolling it out across the organization.

In the end, we significantly improved our client's business condition by using a principles-based approach to growth, adaptable across individual business units. We obtained deep consumer insight and developed and launched numerous new products, with results far exceeding the cost of the study. It was a very favorable return on investment.

GROWTH STRATEGY EVOLUTION

Over twenty years have passed since that initial best practices study. Revisiting our findings today suggests it was a good start. We identified and cataloged many classic tenets of corporate growth—the importance of customer insight, a strong brand, and an innovation mindset. These growth-drivers are foundational to marketing, as important today as they were then.

Still, our initial study had its shortcomings. That work occurred before the emergence of the "digital economy," which, of course, is now just the economy.

Today, business change occurs much faster than it did when leading companies like Apple, Amazon, and Google were in their early stages. Many of the management principles that drive these companies today, including their approaches to product development, organization design, and culture, weren't well understood then.

Certain processes and principles, like rigid, top-down strategy development and a multistage-gate approach to innovation, have largely been replaced. Now, practices like agile planning, design thinking, and minimum viable products (MVP) are proving more effective.

Twenty years ago, customer input came at later and more discrete stages in the product development cycle. Today, it occurs much sooner and in an ongoing fashion. Rigid strategy development that occurred periodically has been replaced with continual listening, learning, and adjusting.

Innovation used to emphasize new products and services. Now, it involves creating new business models and customer experiences, often through digital transformation. Technological innovation, new forms of interactive marketing, and digital disruption are common. Design sprints, rapid prototyping, and digital diaries lead to better, faster, and cheaper innovations.

The way companies and consumers interact has also changed. Historically, marketing communication was mostly one way, from companies to consumers. Now, it's interactive—real-time marketing, including multiple streams of ideas, with continuous strategic strikes.

Brand storytelling and immersive customer experiences have proven more effective than broadcast media in driving sales. Interactive content, personalization, and social and data analytics enable deeper brand-customer relationships.

Increasingly, companies are turning to direct-to-consumer (DTC) marketing as they seek to bypass retailers, wholesalers, and other distributors to serve end customers. Companies that traditionally relied on intermediaries to market and sell their products—including many in the business-to-business space—are now taking the reins in marketing directly to end purchasers.

Marketing, as a concept, has also changed. At one time, marketing was viewed in organizational terms, often as a functional silo. Today, it's seen holistically, from a process perspective, intertwined throughout the organization.

Finally, our initial effort resulted in a listing of growth-focused principles, but it didn't integrate them into a single theme or idea. Although a list of principles is nice, it's still just a list unless the ideas are incorporated into a framework or model.

NEW INSIGHT, NEW PRINCIPLES

Since that time, EquiBrand has worked with scores of client companies across business-to-consumer and business-to-business categories. We've uncovered customer insights, built strong brands, and developed new business models to fuel growth.

In addition to real-world consulting, we continually update our best practice work by adding new companies, challenging assumptions, and pushing, pulling, and refining our thinking, in moving from the *whats* to the *so whats*.

In writing *Upstream Marketing*, we've done a systematic review of seven companies—Amazon, Apple, Google, Nike, Southwest, Starbucks, and The Walt Disney Company—to uncover and illustrate critical upstream concepts.

We've included these seven, collectively referred to as the *profile companies,* based on a variety of factors, including financial performance and access to corporate information through primary and secondary research.

One requirement in selecting our profile companies was growth consistency *over time*. Many of our Silicon Valley startup neighbors, including some we've worked with, show great initial promise only to stumble and fall within a year or two. Our focus is on time-tested, enduring principles.

Throughout the case studies, you'll see surprising consistency in the marketing and innovation principles these profile companies share. Some of the examples may be familiar, especially if you're a student of management thinking. What should be new is perspective *across* these seven organizations, including the standard set of best practices used from their formation as small startups, until now.

For comparison purposes and as a reality check, we also draw on real-world case examples from EquiBrand clients. In some instances, our client cases exemplify best practices. In other cases, we use them to show what *not* to do.

Let's go deeper on upstream marketing, show how it's different from downstream marketing, and introduce the upstream marketing framework, which serves to structure this book.

UPSTREAM MARKETING VS. DOWNSTREAM MARKETING

The idea of going *upstream* to unlock growth is a proven concept, though it lacks familiarity, understanding, structure, and practical instruction. Dr. Ram Charan, a top management consultant, broadly defined the term in his book *Profitable Growth Is Everyone's Business*. There, he talks about the need to "beef up upstream marketing" and describes how downstream differs from upstream this way:

Downstream marketing is what most people visualize as marketing and involves advertising, promotion, brand building, and communicating with customers through public relations, trade shows, and in-store displays. While these activities are extremely important, they tend to enhance the acceptance of a product or service that already exists. Further, companies spend an inordinate amount of money on downstream marketing activities and ignore critical upstream marketing activities.

Upstream marketing, by comparison, refers to the strategic process of identifying and fulfilling customer needs. Upstream marketing takes place at a much earlier stage by developing a clear market segmentation map and then identifying and precisely defining which customer segments to focus on. It analyzes how the end user uses the product or service and what competitive advantage will be required to win the customer and at what price point. This is done very early in the product or service development cycle and is one of the missing links for generating revenue growth at many companies.[2]

Figure 1.1 compares the two stream parts, drawing on EquiBrand's real-world experience to expand on Charan's definition and highlight key differences:

Marketing's Two Streams		
Focus Area	Downstream Marketing	Upstream Marketing
Customer Orientation	A defined target segment, based upon the product or service sold	The entire customer landscape, including new, uncontested market spaces
Growth Areas	Existing products and services with incremental refinements	New products, new channels, and markets, based on obsessive customer insight
Approach	Functionally driven, dependent upon advertising, sales, social media, and PR	Principle-based, built on a set of proven winning practices
Organizing Framework	The Four P's: Product, Place, Price, and Promotion	The Three I's: Insight, Identity, and Innovation
Time Horizon	Short-term, often firefighting	Future-focused (think big, but start small and fail fast)
Planning Cycles	Often either too short (today's crisis) or too long	Around 90 days
Marketing Orientation	"Make people want things"	"Make things people want."

Figure 1.1

In considering upstream and downstream marketing, it's crucial to ensure both are fully aligned and seamlessly integrated. After all, upstream and downstream marketing are different parts of the same stream.

While figure 1.1 shows downstream and upstream side by side, upstream marketing should actually occur first, flowing directly into downstream marketing. Extending the stream analogy, a better visual representation has upstream at the top, splitting into several downstream channels, as in figure 1.2:

Upstream Marketing Leverage

Growth Area #1	Growth Area #2	Growth Area #3

Figure 1.2

Upstream marketing promotes economic leverage: A variety of downstream opportunities emerge from a singular focus on upstream principles. When you start with upstream, downstream flows more smoothly, uncovering multiple opportunities with fewer impediments.

Upstream Marketing Analogy

Here's another way to look at upstream marketing: Ever gone fishing? Think of upstream marketing as everything that happens *before the hook is in the water*. The best anglers reflect and act on several factors before they cast the line. First, they'll consider the kind of fish, the method (fly fishing or bait casting), and the tools needed—the type of rod, reel, fishing line, and so on.

After answering a few other questions—Where exactly will they go to fish, which lake or river? Where within that lake or river? At what time? What's the best bait?—they then bait the hook and cast it into the water.

In doing all this, good anglers observe the essential principles of upstream marketing, thinking through the five W's—*who, what, where, when,* and *why*—before integrating with downstream implementation (sometimes literally) in landing the target.

THE ELUSIVE HEADLINE EMERGES

Amazon, Apple, Google, Nike, Southwest Airlines, Starbucks, and The Walt Disney Company: How have these companies and companies like them been able to consistently grow their business compared with others in their respective industries?

> **The Strongest Brands and Businesses Are Built Upstream Through the Combined Principles of Insight, Identity, and Innovation.**

As different as these companies are in terms of the products and services they offer and markets they serve, their approach and adherence to upstream marketing are remarkably similar. Common to all is emphasis on:

- **Insight:** gaining internal clarity and deep customer understanding as the basis for transformative growth

- **Identity:** building strong value propositions and brands that deliver on customer needs and align with company operations

- **Innovation:** ensuring a continual stream of creative solutions to meet evolving customer needs and expand the business

Leading upstream marketers infuse these principles into everything they do and obtain synergies along the way. If there is a formula for success, it's:

> **Insight + Identity + Innovation = Upstream Marketing**
> **Or 1 + 1 + 1 = 4**

The key to effective upstream marketing is that each principle builds upon the others, reinforcing and magnifying them. Combined, they form an integrated whole much more powerful than the sum of its parts because the principles are all working together, all the time.

Three Factors Distinguish Upstream Marketing Leaders

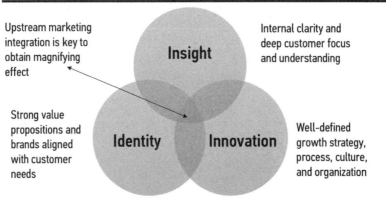

Upstream marketing integration is key to obtain magnifying effect

Internal clarity and deep customer focus and understanding

Strong value propositions and brands aligned with customer needs

Well-defined growth strategy, process, culture, and organization

Figure 1.3

As shown in figure 1.3, insight, identity, and innovation are inextricably linked across all parts of the organization.

For example, insight isn't relegated to the marketing research department. Identity management extends far beyond the walls of the marketing department or ad agency. Innovation is more than an occasional brainstorming session. After years of incorporating these principles into their business models, leading upstream marketers become perpetual insight-identity-innovation machines.

Many organizations *say* they have a similar set of principles, and some do. What distinguishes best-in-class companies are three integrated principles and six related best practices that drive everything they do. As we'll see, each profile company's corporate strategy statements, business processes, company culture, and hiring practices all support the upstream marketing principles.

UPSTREAM MARKETING FRAMEWORK

As companies recognize the differences between upstream and downstream marketing, a new framework and tools for applying insight, identity, and innovation principles and practices are required. The framework, built on EquiBrand's research and in-market client experience, provides the discipline and structure for analyzing and synthesizing results and for organizing the rest of this book.

Think of the upstream marketing framework as a structured way to answer four framing questions: Where to play? How to win? How might we? and What would have to be true? Insight, identity, and innovation serve as *first principles*[1] to direct the approach and help

---

1   * A first principle is a basic assumption that cannot be deduced any further. Many great thinkers, from Aristotle to Elon Musk, use first principle thinking, which involves boiling things down to the fundamental parts that you know to be true and then building up from there. Insight, identity and innovation are the first principles of upstream marketing.

answer the questions. Attached to each principle are two best practices. Finally, underlying the principles and practices is a process to integrate and execute upstream marketing. Figure 1.4 shows the framework, including details describing each component.

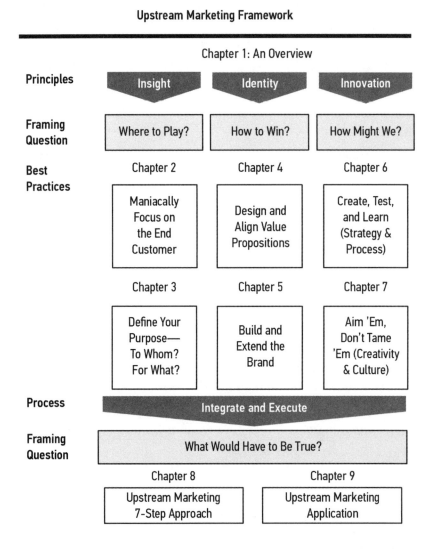

Figure 1.4

While there is order to the framework, don't get hung up on the sequencing and alignment of individual components. The principles, framing questions, and best practices are interrelated and will overlap. For example, the question "What would have to be true?" shown at the bottom of the figure relates to every element of the upstream marketing process.

FOUR FRAMING QUESTIONS

There is a saying that applies to strategy development: "A problem well stated is half solved." When a problem is clearly defined, it's that much easier to answer. Albert Einstein purportedly once said that if he had an hour to solve a problem, he'd spend fifty-five minutes thinking about the problem and five minutes thinking about solutions.

The opposite of this is a concept called "boiling the ocean." As the phrase suggests, if the problem is unclear, there's a risk of trying to do the impossible. Additionally, some issues are so complex, it's difficult to know where to begin, and "analysis paralysis" sets in.

By definition, growth involves new things: new products, new markets, and new channels. Since there's often no existing fact base to consider, it can be unclear how to get started and what comes next. What questions need to be answered to improve success rates?

Management guru Michael Porter sees business strategy as a set of long-term choices that articulate the competitive advantage companies seek to create in order to win. A.G. Lafley, former CEO of Procter & Gamble, and Roger Martin, dean of the Rotman School of Management, echo the strategy-as-choice definition in their book *Playing to Win: How Strategy Really Works*.[3]

Consistent with this approach, questions can be a powerful way to improve upstream marketing. The better the question, the more valuable the answer. Listed here are four interrelated framing questions used in upstream marketing. Each question informs the next and draws on specific methods to obtain answers. Collectively, this Q&A format is vital to structuring the framework. Here are the details:

Where to play? specifically, to whom and for what, is the first strategic business decision to make, regarding where to compete and where not to compete. This involves mapping customer segments (to whom?) and their needs (for what?) to identify strategic opportunity areas. Which customers, markets, channels, and broad product categories should be pursued?

How to win? informs value proposition and brand development. What's the optimal business model, value proposition, product, or service concept to address the specified opportunity area? If *to whom* and *for what* determines the fishing pond, then *how to win* defines the optimal bait.

How might we? jump-starts innovation by pushing for creative solutions to complex problems. Wording the question this way is preferred over "how can we" or "how should we," as it opens up opportunities.[4] This framing question is central to the design sprint process used by Google and other profile companies.

What would have to be true? is the final question that links upstream and downstream marketing. While the first three questions promote expansive thinking, this one narrows choices in moving toward execution. To improve success rates, consider *ahead of time* what's required to win, including business metrics and financial thresholds. Go upstream and use mini tests to assess what must be true about product acceptance, channel penetration, sales, and marketing requirements to succeed. Gain experience before making the next sizable bet.

After considering all these things, keep in mind Porter's other advice for strategy: Define it as "choosing what *not* to do."

Later in this chapter we'll highlight the six best practices that complete the framework (one per chapter). First, though, let's discuss *why* focus on upstream marketing, including key challenges and opportunities to address.

WHY UPSTREAM MARKETING?

The primary reason to pursue upstream marketing is improved business performance. Companies that rapidly identify and reallocate capital to new growth businesses outperform those that take a steady-state approach.[5] When executed well, upstream marketing provides substantial new revenue and profit streams that extend far beyond the core business. Uncontested "white space" market opportunities open up, making competition irrelevant.

After adopting upstream marketing principles and practices, companies tend to look very different than they did in their early stages. The playing field—the customers they serve and the products they deliver—expand significantly.

Imagine if Apple had defined its business in product terms only—as a manufacturer of desktop computers. It would have completely missed out on the revenue associated with the iPod, iPhone, iPad, Apple Watch, Apple TV, and its array of services such as Apple Arcade, Apple Music, TV+, News+, and Card. Today, the combined value of these newer businesses far exceeds that of the original desktop computer portfolio.

Similarly, what if Amazon had remained an online retailer of books only? It's now the world's largest retailer, supplemented by product sales from Kindle, Echo, and a host of other businesses, including self-publishing, groceries, home automation, delivery services, and robotics. Alexa, Amazon Prime, Amazon Music, and Amazon Studios envelop consumers each day. Amazon Web Services (AWS) represents an entirely new business-to-business proposition that contributes significantly to the company's bottom line. Other mega-industries Amazon has its eye on include pharmaceuticals, health care, and financial services.

Disney got its start in animation. Today, it is the largest media company in the world. Studio Entertainment—consisting of all films released by Walt Disney Pictures, Walt Disney Animation Studios, Pixar, Marvel Studios, Lucasfilm, 20th Century Studios, and others—accounts for only 15 percent of total company revenues. The majority of sales and profits comes from its other businesses. Within a year after launching Disney+ in 2019, the company restructured its organization around it to ramp up its direct-to-consumer strategy.[6]

These examples may seem obvious. It's hard to imagine Apple, Amazon, or Disney *not* being as expansive as they are today. And yet many companies—most companies—do what they've been doing from inception. It's why many small businesses remain small businesses. Though not for lack of trying. A study by McKinsey & Company indicates 84 percent of global executives see innovation as extremely important to their growth strategies.[7] Yet a staggering 94 percent are dissatisfied with their organization's innovation performance.

Many companies employ upstream marketing principles in their early stages (perhaps subconsciously) but gradually lose perspective. When launched, they consider choices like to whom, for what, how to win, and other strategic decisions.

Over time, though, day-to-day firefighting often takes over. Along the way, marketing shifts from strategic to tactical. Instead of working *on* the business, execs find themselves working *in* the business.

Despite its proven importance to business success, many business leaders are unfamiliar with upstream marketing. Why is it so neglected? Why do so many companies focus downstream and undervalue upstream marketing? This occurs for several reasons.

UPSTREAM MARKETING CHALLENGES

Upstream marketing is hard to do. Upstream marketing is neither a strategy nor a process but rather a set of principles, framing questions, and underlying practices that need to be consistently applied. Many companies don't know how to get started, or they treat upstream components as separate or distinct, as opposed to an integrated system.

Upstream marketing takes time. Before realizing its benefits, upstream marketing requires thoughtful strategizing, planning, and testing. The payoff in new business is not immediate. Faced with a soft business climate or limited resources, many companies turn to downstream to spur short-term growth and never get around to upstream activities. Upstream is a journey that requires displaying patience and a sense of urgency at the same time.

Upstream marketing lacks tangibility. Downstream efforts like an ad campaign, new website, or slick brochure are often more appealing than a marketing strategy or business plan. It can be challenging to envision the potential value of upstream marketing tools like framing questions, concept statements, and prototypes.

Upstream marketing success can be hard to measure. Sales revenue, ad impressions, click-through rates, lead tracking, and other metrics provide a sense that downstream marketing is working. There are fewer ways to track upstream marketing successes in the short term.

Many organizations are not set up for upstream marketing success. Small to medium-sized businesses may lack the resources and training. Conversely, large organizations may have strategic planning departments staffed with MBAs and data scientists, but these groups are often functionally siloed, disconnected from other functions required to drive growth.

UPSTREAM MARKETING OPPORTUNITIES

There are counterarguments for why upstream marketing makes sense, and why now. The main reason is the substantial business growth that results. New markets, new business models, new products, new channels, and other growth areas open up entirely new revenue streams. Here are other factors:

Customer obsession helps focus the organization. The answers to most marketing strategy questions reside in the marketplace. Companies that invest in deep, proprietary insight about their customers are better equipped and inspired to meet their needs both today and in the future.

Upstream marketing expands the playing field, and creates uncontested market space. Many organizations are driven to hit short-term numbers and therefore fixate on the current state. Be careful. Amazon's Jeff Bezos said, "If everything you do needs to work on a three-year time horizon, then you're competing against a lot of people. But if you're willing to invest on a seven-year time horizon, you're now competing against a fraction of those people, because very few companies are willing to do that."[8]

Upstream marketing offers the opportunity to be "roughly right" rather than "precisely wrong." While precision may be required in certain downstream business practices (in tracking metrics and sales, for example), upstream marketing thrives on being "roughly right." Many business decisions are reversible. Use test-and-learn to minimize the cost of failure. You don't have to win every time, but you need to be in the game. Upstream marketing gets you in the game.

New tools, techniques, and accelerators that support upstream marketing emerge every day. Upstream marketing is more efficient today than in prior years. Agile planning, rapid prototyping, website mock-ups, and 3-D printing are huge time- and cost-savers. New business incubators and entire innovation districts are increasingly available to assist with development.

Consumers are comfortable with the concept of beta products and product updates. Customers have become conditioned to accept products that may not be 100 percent. "Ship and iterate" is an acceptable way tech companies gain early, loyal customers. After version 1, it's 1.1, then 1.2, and eventually version 2.0. Consumers get this, are comfortable with it, and have become more forgiving over time.

With upstream marketing, the Pareto principle (80-20 rule) and Parkinson's law work in combination. The Pareto principle, named after economist Vilfredo Pareto, holds that roughly 80 percent of the effects come from 20 percent of the causes. For example, 80 percent of sales come from 20 percent of your customers, and so on.

Parkinson's law states that "work expands so as to fill the time available." These two ideas become even more powerful when combined. In our experience, companies that integrate a general comfort with ambiguity with a bias for action can reap 90 percent of the benefits of strategic marketing with just 10 percent of the effort.

Upstream marketing combines strategy formulation with execution. There is no centralized planning department, organizational silo or hand-off between functional groups. Rather, upstream marketing is built into strategy from the start and naturally flows to downstream implementation.

BEGIN WITH THE END IN SIGHT

As you'll see, a central theme interwoven throughout this book is *to begin with the end in sight.* This involves envisioning where you want to be in the future and then working backward to fill the gap, using a create-test-and-learn approach.

If you're familiar with Stephen Covey's bestseller, *The 7 Habits of Highly Effective People*, you may see parallels with the second habit, "Begin with the end in mind." This habit involves knowing your purpose and what you're trying to achieve, then using an outcome-oriented mindset to get there.

Said another way, envision what you want in the future and create a plan to get there. Covey explains that with this habit, all things are created twice: first through mental conceptualization and visualization, and second as a physical, actual creation.

Covey's second habit applies to upstream marketing, though with a twist—rather than begin with the end in *mind*, begin with the end in *sight*. It may seem like a subtle distinction, but starting with the end in sight adds another tangible thing to create—a testable proposition, like a concept board, business narrative, draft proposal, or prototype that represents the end goal. In effect, you create things *three* times—first mentally, next as a tangible/testable concept, and finally through actual creation.

By iterating tangible ideas internally and with customers, you can peer into the future, clarify thinking, optimize ideas, reset—as necessary—and get everyone on the same page.

This is why Disney creates storyboards and models in planning new attractions, why Amazon requires business leaders to create six-page narratives (not PowerPoint slides) to debate ideas internally, and why Nike iteratively develops and tests prototypes with professional athletes.

Most innovations fail. The root cause is the inability to accurately define the end state at the beginning. Starting with the end in sight and working backward allows for better decisions about what to do and how to do it. Clarify this upfront so people engage. And remember: If you can't clearly express an idea ahead of time, you may not have an idea.

HOW THIS BOOK IS ORGANIZED

The rest of the book draws on the winning strategic patterns of the profile companies contained in the upstream framework (see Figure 1.4). Here's a preview of what's to come.

Principle 1: Insight. Internal clarity and proprietary customer insight are foundational to upstream marketing. Here we describe the role insight plays in strategy development and specific ways to obtain it.

- **Chapter 2: Maniacally Focus on the End Customer.** Google considers itself an engineering company; Amazon, a retailer; Disney, a media and entertainment company. Dig deeper, though, and the unifying element is their commitment to customer-centricity.

Upstream marketers define their markets in customer terms and obsess about the customer experience. Here we introduce a step-by-step approach and practical tips to obtain customer clarity.

- **Chapter 3: Define Your Purpose—To Whom? For What?** Along with a commitment to insight, every organization needs a clear sense of purpose to direct strategy, including where and how to compete. An organization's purpose, when linked with a customer demand framework, provides the structure to identify strategic opportunity areas. In formulaic terms:

> **To whom + For what = Strategic opportunity area**

This focus allows expert marketers to pursue initial beachhead targets, demonstrate success, and expand the business over time.

Principle 2: Identity. Your identity is who you are, and establishing it should start internally—first, define your purpose, then prove that identity externally. Mission, vision, and value statements are essential components, though are not enough. You need two critical aspects—value propositions and brand strategy—to win.

- **Chapter 4: Design and Align Value Propositions.** Winning marketers create a multidimensional definition of value, aligning customer needs, benefit planks, and company operations. They employ creativity and concept iteration to identify new market spaces and then work backward to deliver solutions.

- **Chapter 5: Build and Extend the Brand.** It's no surprise the seven profile companies top the list of the most valued brands. Historically managed by ad agencies, brand is now a strategic weapon senior executives use to increase corporate value. They know how to build a deep, shared meaning of the brand internally and with customers externally, to craft and manage a portfolio of brands, and to selectively extend them to new areas.

Principle 3: Innovation. This is the hallmark of upstream marketing, and leading organizations draw on it to consistently fuel growth. We break innovation down into two core components: those dealing with strategy and process, and those relating to creativity and culture.

- **Chapter 6: Create, Test, and Learn (Strategy & Process).** Each profile company has its own innovation process, though they share common elements. Guided by insight and identity, the companies use similar methods—focused ideation, iterative concept development, prototyping, business screening—to open new opportunity areas.

- **Chapter 7: Aim 'Em, Don't Tame 'Em (Creativity & Culture).** While organizational and cultural issues are often dismissed or overlooked as "soft stuff," these are the very things that distinguish successful upstream marketers. The phrase, "aim 'em, don't tame 'em," coined by strategic facilitator Cavas Gobhai, encapsulates the seemingly contradictory values and behaviors needed to drive growth.[9]

Now Apply It: Integrate and Execute. Any upstream marketing principle alone can improve business performance. Implementing them holistically unlocks their true potential. Insight informs identity, which improves innovation, which enhances insight, and the process repeats. It's not a single thing. It's all of them working together.

- **Chapter 8: Upstream Marketing 7-Step Approach.** Upstream marketing principles are universal. The method for enacting them, however, varies. What works for one company may not for another. To jump-start upstream marketing, we share a proven seven-step approach. We show how integration—including active participation of executive decision makers at crucial points—is critical for success.

- **Chapter 9: Upstream Marketing Application.** Would your organization benefit from an increased focus on upstream marketing? We complete the framework with case examples and a set of questions to diagnose the potential impact.

Terms and Definitions

Companies use different words to describe their end purchasers, including buyers, candidates, clients, consumers, customers, guests, members, patrons, prospects, and users. For purposes of this book, we use the terms *consumer* and *customer* interchangeably to encompass the ultimate buyer of goods and services across industries. We also consider these terms to include both current customers and non-customer prospects.

Upstream marketing is a concept that extends beyond what many view as marketing. The term *upstream marketer* is designed to be inclusive across titles, functional groups, and skill sets in strategy, marketing, sales, product development, research and development (R&D), and others.

Exactly who leads upstream efforts can vary. In large corporations, this could be the chief executive officer, chief marketing officer, or chief experience officer. In small to medium-sized businesses, it might be the business owner or marketing manager.

In this book, the sequence unfolds in the following order—insight, identity, and innovation. In reality, the order could switch, beginning with identity or innovation and mixing in the others. The sequence doesn't matter, provided the principles are all understood and delivered at the same time.

Likewise, the four framing questions—where to play, how to win, how might we, and what would have to be true—tend to align with the four parts of the book—insight, identity, innovation, and integration. There is, however, iteration and overlap, so you can ask the four framing questions at any time. Consider them back-pocket questions to structure thinking and facilitate decision making whenever useful.

Innovation can take many forms, including new company formation, new business models, extended value propositions, new offerings, new products and services, and changes in business capabilities and operations. Upstream marketing has broad application, and for clarity here, we often use the phrase *new products* to encompass a range of innovation forms.

Finally, for illustration purposes, client cases draw mostly from consumer categories understood by a broad audience. That said, the principles and practices work across complex categories—commercial banking and financial securities, risk management, medical devices, biopharmaceutical products, specialty pharma, computer hardware, software and services, and others. Don't let the simplicity of the cases detract from the importance of the lessons. See chapter 9 for more involved case examples.

GO UPSTREAM

After years of helping companies grow, our research and experience indicate that the root cause of moderate or stalled growth is an overreliance on downstream marketing.

Many companies see their business as largely fixed and focus on the wrong problem, using downstream marketing tactics to fight it out with competitors and eke out the last bit of sales revenue or profit contribution. Downstream is needed, but it's not enough.

Despite what management consultants, research companies, ad agencies, and marketing software providers might say, there is no single solution to growth. Psychologist Abraham Maslow said, "I suppose it is tempting, if the only tool you have is a hammer, to treat everything as if it were a nail." A one-off solution is the wrong approach.

Going upstream offers the opportunity for sustainable brand and business growth. Effective execution, though, involves doing many things well. It requires that the entire organization understand, adopt, and adhere to three universal principles and six best practices. Let's get started with insight, the first principle.

QUESTIONS TO CONSIDER

1. Does the C-suite view the business playing field as largely fixed, or is it open to redefining the landscape?

2. Does your organization understand the critical differences between upstream and downstream marketing?

3. Are adequate resources being allocated to upstream marketing?

PRINCIPLE 1

Insight

INSIGHT

ASK A GROUP OF A half dozen marketers to define the term "marketing" and you'll likely get a dozen or more answers. Most will agree marketing is a broad topic, involves both art and science, and covers a wide range of activities in growing a business.

While there are literally hundreds of definitions of marketing, here's a simple one that fits our purposes: *Marketing is meeting wants and needs profitably.*

Of course, to meet needs, you have to understand them first, and that is the role of insight. As we see in the next couple of chapters, insight promotes clarity. The more clearly you define your organization's purpose and understand your customers, the better success you'll have.

Chapter 2: Maniacally Focus on the End Customer defines insight and provides an overarching approach to structure market research inputs and outputs. Here we introduce proven ways to obtain insight, including how-to tips to experiment and learn.

Chapter 3: Define Your Purpose—To Whom? For What? describes how to integrate internal clarity with customer understanding. Internally, start with *why* and define your organization's aspiration. Then, establish a customer management framework (to whom and for what) in determining strategic growth areas.

Asking the right questions in the right sequence results in better, faster, and cheaper answers. The next two chapters show you how.

CHAPTER 2

MANIACALLY FOCUS ON THE END CUSTOMER

"The best vision is insight."
—Malcolm Forbes, *entrepreneur and publisher*

"Creativity and insight almost always involve an experience of acute pattern recognition: the eureka moment in which we perceive the interconnection between disparate concepts or ideas to reveal something new."
—Jason Silva, *filmmaker and futurist*

"Nothing is more terrible than activity without insight."
—Thomas Carlyle, *historian and essayist*

SINCE THE LAUNCH OF ITS first computer in the late 1970s, Apple has met customer needs like no other company. In the process, it defined and redefined entire industries.

Personal computers, digital music players, mobile phones, tablets, and home automation all existed before the Mac, iPod, iPhone, iPad or HomePod. Apple didn't invent most of the products it offers. What Apple did was simplify technology and deliver new things in new ways.

While consumers may *say* they want extra features, Apple knows that too many bells and whistles overcomplicate and can detract from higher-order benefits of ease and simplicity. Apple's secret is satisfying needs customers don't even know they have.

Steve Jobs explained Apple's customer focus this way: "And as we have tried to come up with a strategy and a vision for Apple, it started with 'What incredible benefits can we give to the customer? Where can we take the customer?' Not starting with 'Let's sit down with the engineers and figure out what awesome technology we have and then how are we going to market that?' And I think that's the right path to take."[10] Apple became successful by flipping the orientation of traditional, technology-driven industries to be consumer- rather than technology-driven.

Walt Disney's idea to build Disneyland occurred to him while sitting on a park bench watching his daughters ride a merry-go-round at a local amusement park. He felt disconnected from his daughters and wanted to participate in the experience. Disney said, "What this country really needs is an amusement park that families can take their children to."[11] Walt's insight: develop an amusement park that parents and children could *enjoy together*.

Over the next decade, Walt visited a dozen or so different parks for inspiration before launching Disneyland.

According to Disney animator Ollie Johnston "Walt was very thorough, and he really looked into this stuff." Said Walt, "When we consider a new project, we really study it—not just the surface idea, but everything about it."[12]

Walt's use of insight and creativity resulted in two new disciplines at Disney—Guestology, for uncovering consumer insights, and Imagineering, fusing imagination with engineering to create innovative experiences. These disciplines are still in practice today, allowing the company to stay close to consumers while creating magical attractions.

Google was founded on *technical* insight into how website links underlie the importance of individual pages. Much of its business success is based on *consumer insight*. While competitors were creating portals to attract consumers and advertisers, Google resisted the temptation and kept its homepage clear and simple.

The insight? The more time users spent *outside* of its own site, the more money it made through pay-per-click ads. Former CEO Eric Schmidt said, "We focus on quality, and we have a very simple model. If we show fewer ads that are more targeted, those ads are worth more. So, we're in this strange situation where we show a smaller number of ads and we make more money because we show better ads. And that's the secret of Google."[13]

All of these companies place a premium on asking and answering the right questions. Often, customer clarity leads to counterintuitive business decisions: Competitors head down one path, while the profile companies pursue another direction or chart a new course entirely. Superior insight provides the platform for competitive advantage.

INSIGHT—THE OVERLOOKED PRINCIPLE

Do an online search for "top global brands" or "most innovative companies" and you'll see a variety of annual published rankings. The same companies are often at the top, including a subset of the profile companies. Yet, in a principles-based approach to growth, insight, identity, and innovation are equally important. Where, then, is the published list of insight leaders? It doesn't exist, at least not on paper.

Insight is an often overlooked principle mainly because it lacks tangibility. It's relatively easy to quantify innovation and brand identity strength. New product revenues, market share, stock price, and statistical surveys can be evaluated.

Not so with insight. Deep, proprietary understanding may exist within the minds and file folders of the company, its leaders, and employees—but it doesn't show up, at least explicitly, on a company's balance sheet.

The true value of customer obsession and insight is the role it plays in brand and business model evolution. Insight is merely a means to an end, and only results in economic benefits when it's combined with identity and innovation.

Just because you can't see or quantify insight, though, doesn't mean it's not important. Our work with leading upstream marketers indicates it is *the* underlying, driving component of their success. Along with defining the organization's purpose and high-level growth strategy, insight is the first step. An outside-in perspective is required to counteract the bias of internal focus. Let's go deeper into what insight is and how to obtain it.

WHAT IS INSIGHT?

Insight is the ability to understand something in a very clear way by gaining an almost intuitive understanding of the situation. Insight goes beyond knowledge and understanding to uncover the *whys* and strategic implications. It's the "aha" or "eureka" moment when knowledge and understanding come together. Knowledge and understanding provide the dots. Insight connects the dots. This chart describes this relationship:

FROM INFORMATION TO INSIGHT ➤		
Knowledge (What)	**Understanding (How)**	**Insight (Why)**
Perception	Comprehension	Resolution
Facts	Meaning	Implication
Information	Principles	Application
Memory	Reason	Action

Here's another definition—knowledge is measuring that a desert path is 12.4 miles long. Understanding is packing enough water for the hike. Insight is building a lemonade stand at mile six.[14]

Three Types of Insight

Let's extend this desert path/lemonade stand example to highlight three different types of insight—customer, marketplace, and technical. Each type is needed, and their intersection leads to growth. Here's how an adept upstream marketer might gather insight on each type for a lemonade stand in the desert.

For *customer insight*, consider the wants and needs of end customers, in this case, hikers. Interview or observe them. Better yet, conduct ethnographic research—hike along with them and immerse yourself in their situation. What might they seek in a refreshment stand offering, and why? Asking *why* opens up broader opportunities. Is the need lemonade, or is it really quenching thirst and rehydration?

For *marketplace insight*, study situational factors like the physical path, its environment, and other aspects surrounding the journey. Focus on macro-level issues, including competitive assessment, trend analysis, and desk research. Don't be overly concerned with competitors, but be aware: If another company secures building rights for a retail outlet at mile-marker 5.8, that's important to know.

Finally, invest in *technological insight* to define how to create innovative solutions in a new way. Technical insights might include food chemistry, logistics, cooling systems, solar energy, and drone delivery. How can technical solutions be combined to devise new offerings?

Now, analyze and synthesize the perspectives and iteratively develop and optimize potential solutions. Experiment to learn. Your first recipe for lemonade might be too sweet for thirsty customers; make a small batch of a low-sugar recipe and test how they like it instead. This process is the essence of insight applied to business decision making.

> Trends analysis, a particular type of marketplace insight, helps signal the future state. Trends can occur at macro- and industry-specific levels. One of the biggest trends affecting many categories today is a shift in direct-to-consumer (DTC) marketing, as companies seek to bypass retailers, wholesalers, and other distributors to serve end customers.
>
> Other macro trends include the use of artificial intelligence and machine learning. Jeff Bezos said, "These big trends are not that hard to spot (they get talked and written about a lot), but they can be strangely hard for large organizations to embrace."[15] The important thing is to stay on top of trends and embrace them quickly.

The key to obtaining deep, proprietary insight? Look closer and think deeper.

Look Closer, Think Deeper

There is a great scene in the movie *Dead Poets Society* when the character played by the late Robin Williams, English teacher John Keating, stands on his desk during one of his lectures. He challenges his students to look beyond the ordinary.

"Why do I stand up here? I stand upon my desk to remind myself that we must constantly look at things in a different way. You see the world looks very different from up here. Don't believe me? Come see for yourself. Just when you think you know something; you have to look at it in another way. Even though it may seem silly or wrong, you must try."

The scene ends with the following directive: "Break out. Don't just walk off the desk like lemmings. Look around you. Dare to strike out and find new ground."[16]

The lesson is twofold and applies to the principle of insight: First, change your perspective. If you look at the world like everyone else, you will see the same things. Second, find new territories—uncover and identify new opportunities. Look closer. Think deeper. Maniacal focus and new perspective is the recipe for clarity and insight.

Apple's Steve Jobs held similar views: "Creativity is just connecting things. When you ask creative people how they did something, they feel a little guilty because they didn't really do it, they just saw something. It seemed obvious to them after a while. That's because they were able to connect experiences they've had and synthesize new things. And the reason they were able to do that was that they've had more experiences, or they have thought more about their experiences than other people. Unfortunately, that's too rare a commodity. A lot of people in our industry haven't had very diverse experiences. So, they don't have enough dots to connect, and they end up with very linear solutions without a broad perspective on the problem. The broader one's understanding of the human experience, the better design we will have."[17]

Obtain Deep, Proprietary, and Actionable Insights

Collecting the same customer information, in the same way, won't cut it. In our consulting work, we ask a critical question: *What do you know about your important customers that your competitors don't know?*

We used to consider this question hypothetically. Over time, though, we've found real value in having clients list, one by one, proprietary insights. The initial reaction is often blank stares, as many people have trouble putting pen to paper. Others admit they don't know. More in-touch team members vigorously scribble or type in their answers. We then probe responses: Who are your most valuable customers? How do we define your competitive set? How do we make deep understanding actionable?

Here's one way to obtain deep insight, taken from a client case example:

ETHNOGRAPHIC RESEARCH— THE DEPRIVATION STUDY

This engagement involved identifying new growth opportunities for a leading manufacturer of backpacks, including developing new products and extending the brand into related categories. Ethnographic research was used to understand how students use their daypacks for school.

A brilliant stage of the research, dubbed, "The Deprivation Study," involved taking kids' backpacks away for one week. That's right. They were asked to go about their lives as usual, but without their daypacks.

Researchers then followed the teens throughout the day to understand their lifestyles, values, and the role backpacks played in their lives, including the emotional connection they had with their packs.

The research also provided insight into friction points, including the features and functions that constituted the ideal pack. The sessions were filmed and analyzed and shared throughout the organization.

Later, the client applied its technical insight—in fabrics, materials, compression science, and load balancing—to design a line of new backpacks to better meet customer needs.

This insight helped the company look at the business from a different perspective, through a different lens. Identifying and eliminating customer friction points is one of the surest ways to innovation success. This requires disproving common assumptions, and the best way to do this is by asking different and better questions.

Market Research vs. Customer Obsession

Market research can *lead* to insight, but on its own, it is not insight. Many strong marketers dismiss traditional research. Despite the importance Steve Jobs placed on intuitive insight, he was proud Apple did little market research, saying, "It's really hard to design products by focus groups. A lot of times, people don't know what they want until you show it to them."[18]

Similarly, Starbucks' Howard Schultz said, "I despise research. I think it's a crutch."[19]

Jeff Bezos from Amazon looks at it this way: "Good inventors and designers deeply understand their customer. They spend tremendous energy developing that intuition. They study and understand many anecdotes rather than only the averages you'll find on surveys. They *live* with the design.

"I'm not against beta testing or surveys. But you, the product or service owner, must understand the customer, have a vision, and love the offering. Then, beta testing and research can help you find your blind spots. A remarkable customer experience starts with heart, intuition, curiosity, play, guts, taste. You won't find any of it in a survey."[20]

These business leaders obsess about customers and insight but disregard traditional market research. Why? In our experience, many companies view market research in narrow terms, as a proxy for insight, anchored downstream and in the past.

A lot of market research sees things through the rearview mirror: What happened *yesterday*? How did sales perform in Topeka compared with a year ago? How many social media likes did the latest blog post generate? Also, a lot of existing data is descriptive regarding the *whats* and the *hows*. What are customers doing, and how have they behaved historically? This information does little to uncover growth opportunity areas.

The key is to immerse yourself in the customer experience, take a forward-looking windshield perspective, and focus on the *whys*. Your end goal should be clarity of thought that inspires action.

We sometimes hear from clients, "We didn't learn anything new" after conducting primary research interviews. We respectfully indicate the question isn't, "Did you hear anything new?" It's "Did you hear anything you're not currently addressing?" And, more importantly, "Why aren't you addressing it?" Don't confuse market research with applied insight. Customer insight must be integrated with action to unlock growth.

TURNING INSIGHT INTO ACTION

Occasionally we'll get a call from a potential client who values customer input but is unsure how to obtain it. "We want to conduct research" is the request. We follow up with probing questions to understand their needs better. To whom do you want to talk, and for what purpose?

There are a variety of ways to uncover insight. The method used should flow from the questions you want answers to, whether formally, through market research, or informally, by immersing yourself in the customer experience.

Also, different research techniques are useful at different times. The optimal flow moves from broad to narrow, alternating between qualitative and quantitative methods. This approach allows for analysis (breaking down) and synthesis (building up) to increase certainty and improve strategic decision making.

Two broad types of customer insight are used in determining where to play and informing how to win.

Where to play insight, as described in the next chapter, involves identifying strategic opportunity areas (SOAs) to focus growth. Conventional where to play research techniques include exploratory research and market segmentation.

How-to-win insight, often tied to a ninety-day project development cycle, involves doing a deep dive to uncover and study solutions to a particular problem or SOA. Immerse yourself in the customer situation and then use test-and-learn, concept iteration to develop new business models, value propositions, products, and services (see figure 2.1).

Customer Insight in Upstream Marketing

Type	WHERE TO PLAY			HOW TO WIN	
Scope	Strategic Direction Setting			Concept Optimization	
Role	Segment the market to obtain proprietary insight and identify strategic opportunities			Conduct a "deep dive" and use concept iteration to meet target customer needs	
Process	**Sequential**			**Iterative—Create, Test, & Learn**	
	Understand the Situation	Segment the Market	Confirm Strategic Opportunity Areas		
Method	Qualitative	Quantitative		Qualitative	Quantitative
Research Type	Exploratory	Segmentation		CORE	Validation
Timing	Both foundational (segmentation every 3 – 5 years) and ongoing (continuous listening)			Tied to business cycles, i.e., 90-day increments, including continual iterations	
Viewpoint	Broad ⟵————————————————————⟶ Narrow				

Figure 2.1

Quantitative and qualitative research used to be costly and take weeks or months to complete. New web-based methods, including digital diaries and online ethnography studies, can now be fielded in days or weeks at a fraction of the cost. While the digital research methods differ, the principles remain the same.

In moving from where to play to how to win, insight should become more detailed and produce greater decision-making confidence. This broad-to-narrow, qualitative-to-quantitative pattern works across industries, from consumer goods to business-to-business categories.

A Consumer Product Example

Ever eat pancakes at home? If so, do you make them from scratch, use a mix, or eat the frozen kind? Does adding water to the mix constitute baking? How about adding an egg? We set out to answer these and other questions for a client looking to grow their business through upstream marketing.

The client manufactures baking mixes for pancakes, waffles, cakes, muffins, and other products. Growth had stalled due to changes in consumer eating habits, increased competition, new product failures, and a lack of consumer insight.

The challenge? Stimulate growth by segmenting the market, solidifying the brand positioning, and identifying new products. It was a classic case of deciding where to play, and how to win.

We began the project by conducting internal interviews and performing a three C's analysis (for consumers, company, and competitors insight) to confirm the situation and identify learning gaps. This involved reviewing consumer trends—including their desire for convenience, portability, and flavor variety—and obtaining brand-specific insight.

We also developed a four-part research plan to learn from consumers. Here's an overview of each type of insight gathered and the client issues addressed.

Exploratory insight helps *explain* and *frame* key aspects of the consumer and category. This insight is foundational and plays a role in segmenting the market, uncovering customer needs, establishing customer journey maps, and identifying potential new market spaces. Focus on understanding the *what*s and *why*s. Questioning starts broad—what are customer needs, motivations, attitudes, and friction points?—then narrows in on potential solutions. Methods include in-depth customer interviews, digital diaries, and ethnographic research.

With our baking mix client, we explored different types of cooking (from scratch, mixes, and other options) and how consumers viewed various solutions.

Since our client positioned its brand relative to homemade baking ("homemade made easy"), including the "just add water" product claim, we needed to understand a few things from consumers: How do you define homemade? Does adding ingredients change your view?

Like most categories, the answers varied by the consumers, providing insight into segmentation opportunities.

Segmentation insight splits consumers into different groups based on their attitudes, motivations, and needs. This understanding is obtained both qualitatively and quantitatively and informs customer framework development and portfolio management opportunities.

This structure allowed us to put stakes in the ground and avoid "boiling the ocean." Based on the exploratory research, we identified four "to whom" segments, breaking out 100 hypothetical consumers into four groups:

- *Homemade bakers* who like to cook from scratch. They're willing to invest time and effort, believing that baking with mixes is basic and boring, even causing them a little guilt.

- *Mix enthusiasts* who also love to cook, and view baking mixes as a way to save time.

- *Reluctant bakers* who don't enjoy baking but do it out of a sense of obligation for their kids and family.

- *Baking avoiders* who rarely bake, as they consider it a hassle. They prefer to eat ready-to-eat or frozen baked goods.

To test a useful, hypothesized framework, ask the following questions: Can you see yourself or others you know in the solution? Does it make sense on a gut level? If not, strive for a better, more meaningful answer.

Drawing on our hypothesized demand framework, we then created an online survey for even more precision. Through statistical analysis, a fifth consumer group emerged that divided mix users into two distinct groups—an enthusiastic baker segment and a slightly guilty mix user.

We also tested and identified several "for what" need states within the baking category. For example, one need related to the breakfast occasion of getting family members up and out the door during the week (a great fit for frozen, microwavable, and portable breakfast items). Another related to "big breakfast" occasions, often on weekends, where baking from scratch or mixes offered an element of sociability.

Mapping the to-whom consumer segments with the for-what need states yielded distinct strategic opportunity areas, including several new demand spaces. Our project then shifted to obtain insight on new product solutions, developed using focused ideation and prototyping, through the Concept Optimization REsearch (or CORE) process.

CORE insight uses concept stimuli to obtain market feedback on new products, brand positioning, and messaging ideas. Which ideas are most relevant and why? The goal is to define the end state through a create-test-and-learn approach. Develop a surplus of ideas and optimize them before investing in full development.

Testable concepts—written statements, website mock-ups, and physical prototypes—are exposed to customers to iterate the concepts and narrow the list. Figure 2.2 provides an overview.

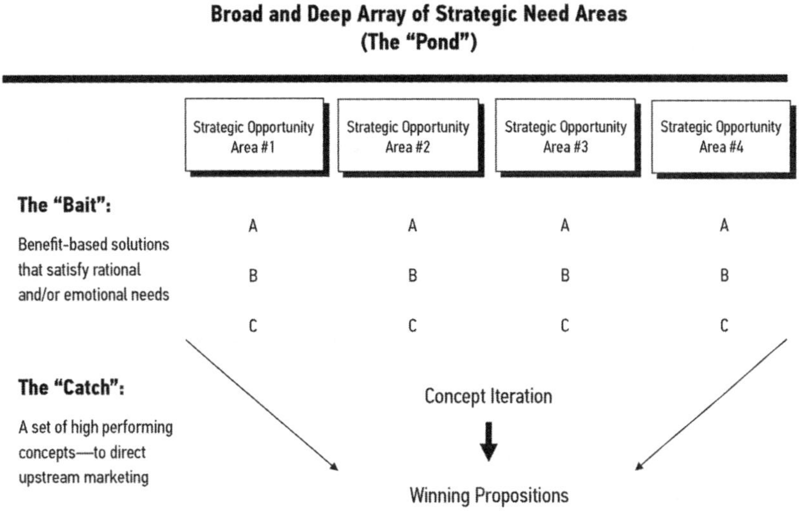

**Broad and Deep Array of Strategic Need Areas
(The "Pond")**

	Strategic Opportunity Area #1	Strategic Opportunity Area #2	Strategic Opportunity Area #3	Strategic Opportunity Area #4
The "Bait": Benefit-based solutions that satisfy rational and/or emotional needs	A B C	A B C	A B C	A B C

The "Catch":

A set of high performing concepts—to direct upstream marketing

Concept Iteration

↓

Winning Propositions

Figure 2.2

The CORE approach differs from traditional concept development in a few ways.

First, rather than cultivate only one area, develop a range of ideas—from closer in to further out—tied to different benefit-based strategic areas (represented in the figure as Strategic Opportunity Areas 1, 2, 3, and 4). In this way, concept development is like adopting a venture capitalist mindset rather than a startup mentality. Use a *portfolio approach* to address multiple opportunities and challenges instead of anchoring on a single idea. Consider multiple fishing ponds.

Second, the CORE approach involves developing multiple ideas *within* a single benefit area (ideas A, B, and C). For example, the benefit of convenience or simplicity can be expressed in various ways—time savings, ease of use, automation, or a single-source solution. Use tangible concepts as bait.

Finally, concept iteration replaces the traditional yes/no stage-gate approach to innovation. As ideas progress, they undergo continual refinement in moving closer to launch and learn. Target and hook the catch.

With our baking mix client, we tested a control concept and then a range of new ideas, including positioning and product ideas that went beyond "just add water" to include other ingredients. Here's the control concept.

BRAND X. HOMEMADE MADE EASY

You don't always have the time to make your pancakes and baked goods from scratch, but with Brand X mixes, you can still enjoy the warmth of home baking. Brand X is homemade made easy, authentic recipes brought to life with high-quality ingredients and care. Our just-add-water pancake mixes and muffins, pies, dessert bars are all homemade, but without all the *time* of homemade.

Over time, we changed, added, dropped, and combined concepts as a result of target feedback. As it turns out, for example, having consumers add an egg to the product mix in addition to water greatly enhanced the concept appeal with the guilty mix users group.

Validation insight is the final step, often using quantitative research to determine what's required to successfully market the new offering. As product concepts take shape, you may need to make trade-offs in finalizing the offering, pricing, and preparing to launch. What product features are most appealing at which price point? A variety of statistical techniques are available, and these methods begin to transition to downstream marketing as they move toward implementation.

There you have it—four insight-gathering methods that, when combined, inform and help answer to whom and for what, how to win, how might we, and what would have to be true.

Actual insight-gathering methods will, of course, vary by company, as shown in the next example from Disney. The general approach, though, is consistent across profile companies.

WHAT WOULD HAVE TO BE TRUE TO PROCEED WITH DISNEYLAND?

Walt Disney applied a similar insight-gathering approach in deciding whether to move forward with the Disneyland concept. While his methods varied, he fully immersed his team in the amusement park category. He used exploratory research, including visiting as many parks as he could, to define the new market space and to see what worked and what didn't. He used market segmentation to target a specific consumer type—families—and *not* traditional amusement park goers. Kids *and* parents (or kids at heart) were the Disney target consumers.

Initial exploratory work and targeting decisions inspired early park ideas, which were expressed in concept drawings and models. From Disneylandia to Mickey Mouse Park to Disneyland, ideas underwent extensive refinement, drawing on internal and external feedback.

Throughout the development process, Walt researched and sought expert opinions to inform what would have to be true. This included conducting a focus group with other park operators during an annual amusement park industry convention and trade show held in Chicago.

The consensus among Walt's contemporaries about his idea? It wouldn't work. It was too impractical and overly costly to produce. Walt valued their feedback and said he'd consider their input, but the session actually confirmed for him that he wanted to move forward with Disneyland.

"Rather than being dissuaded, he was even more certain that his idea would work. Instead of another amusement park, Walt knew he was creating the first theme park."[21] Walt knew certain things needed to be true before proceeding with Disneyland. This insight validated those conditions.

Walt ultimately decided on a simple, inspiring concept statement to articulate his vision:

> "Physically, Disneyland would be a small world in itself. It would encompass the essence of the things that were good and true in American life. It would reflect the faith and challenge of the future, the entertainment, the interest in intelligently presented facts, the stimulation of the imagination, the standards of health and achievement, and above all, a sense of strength, contentment and well-being."[22]

This original concept statement, developed over sixty-five years ago, continues to influence The Walt Disney Company brand and business today.

TIPS FOR OBTAINING PROPRIETARY INSIGHT

In our consulting work, we begin every client engagement by defining what is known and unknown about the customer, market, and current situation.

Some organizations have a staggering amount of market intelligence. In others, it's virtually nonexistent. You'd think the more customer research, the better the insight. Often, the opposite is true. Many clients overspend and are overwhelmed by research. Other clients are starved for insight, misinterpret data, and make poor inferences.

In any case, it's vital to assess what is known before gathering new insights. So, start by gathering inputs—research reports, social media tracking, sales force input, and industry studies.

Analyze large data sets using artificial intelligence and other methods to reveal patterns and trends relating to consumer behavior.

Then, interview managers and synthesize the findings. Create an initial fact base, formulate hypotheses, and identify gaps to fill. To connect the dots, you need to have the dots.

With the existing foundation set, prepare an insights-gathering plan using figure 2.1 on page 43. Consider the following seven tips for looking closer and thinking deeper.

Tip 1: Be Clear About Who You're Obtaining Insight From.

Sometimes, a broad range of perspectives is essential for strategic context. In other cases, do a "deep dive" with a particular segment.

Gaining broad insight *across* groups provides a complete picture of the market. This is best for exploratory work when canvassing the market or developing hypotheses for the customer demand framework, as described in the next chapter.

Within the automotive category, for example, different consumers value different things. Some drivers see their vehicles as a way to get from point A to point B, and others see their cars as an extension of themselves. Having a total market view provides context and helps narrow in on the best opportunities.

Often, you can obtain clarity by doing a deep dive with highly involved "power users" and "extreme consumers." Not all customers are of equal value, and there is a risk to treating them this way.

In many categories, the 80-20 rule applies: 20 percent of customers account for 80 percent of the sales. These "power users" are the most involved, set the highest standards, provide richer insight, and tend to be more profitable. It pays to understand and keep them happy.

Another group to consider is "extreme consumers." These consumers lie "in the tails" of a standard bell curve and offer perspective outside the mainstream, on the cutting edge.

Automotive enthusiasts, foodies, fashionistas, Disneyphiles, a cult of Mac followers, and other extreme consumers can provide valuable insight and signal early opportunities with eventual mainstream impact.

MINI CASE EXAMPLE

We were hired by a nutritional supplements company to help "mainstream" their core product—microalgae. The company's products sold well with certain consumers—from marathoners and ironman competitors to vegans and natural nutritionists. While the client wanted to target a mass-market consumer, this segment didn't know the first thing about supplements, other than natural foods were "on trend" and good for them. Rather than research only average consumers, we also obtained deep insight from extreme consumers who shopped at natural food health stores and then translated the benefits sought to a broader group. Mainstream consumers aspired to eat healthier, so we took our insight cues from the most involved consumer segments.

Finally, in identifying new market and brand development spaces, make sure to talk to both current customers and non-customers. Current customers provide valuable insight into their needs and why they have bonded with your brands. Prospects help identify pain points, barriers to acceptance, and market expansion opportunities.

Tip 2: Focus on Customer Benefits, Jobs to Be Done and New Demand Spaces Rather Than Product Attributes.

"People don't want to buy a quarter-inch drill; they want a quarter-inch hole."[23] This quote by Theodore Levitt, American economics and business professor, speaks to the idea of focusing on customer benefits rather than product attributes.

In his landmark *Harvard Business Review* article, "Marketing Myopia," Levitt urged companies to define their industries more broadly than they might otherwise. This provides the platform for creating and capturing uncontested market spaces. He argued, for example, that the railroad industry got in trouble because industry leaders presumed they were in the railroad rather than the transportation business. They were product-oriented instead of customer-oriented. While product attributes come and go, consumer benefits are more enduring.

EXAMPLES OF MARKETING MYOPIA

Numerous examples exist where companies and entire industries collapsed because of failure to meet target needs. These companies focused on product attributes, not customer benefits (or jobs to be done), and lost out to new competitors.

Consider the evolution of the recording industry. First, there were phonographs, then LPs, and further changes from 8-track tapes to cassette tapes, compact discs, MiniDiscs, MP3s, and other digital audio formats, and audio streaming.

The insight? Consumers want convenient access to music and are mostly indifferent to how it's delivered.

As consumers demanded better quality and greater convenience, companies focusing solely on product attributes and technical specs instead of underlying customer needs were replaced. Companies that remained focused on the recording format (LPs, discs, etc.) or the device that played them (record players, cassette players, etc.), and not the end benefit, ceased to be viable.

Innovation tends to follow a benefit-based, problem-solution format: Necessity is the mother of invention. In developing and marketing new products, consider the compromises customers and non-customers make within the category. Then, create concepts to solve these problems. Sometimes, it's less about *problems* and more about *opportunities*. The terms "pain points" and "gain points" are used to recognize this problem/opportunity dynamic.

A related idea of focusing on customer benefits is solving customer friction points or jobs to be done (JTBD). A JTBD, made popular by Harvard Business School professor Clayton Christensen, is not a product, service, or a specific solution. It's the customer's higher purpose. The key is to understand the "job" customers have and explore alternative solutions.

Consider Apple's launch of the first iPod. Note the headline of the press release referencing the job to be done, putting 1,000 songs in your pocket.

APPLE PRESENTS IPOD
Ultra-Portable MP3 Music Player
Puts 1,000 Songs in Your Pocket

CUPERTINO, California—October 23, 2001—Apple® today introduced iPod™, a breakthrough MP3 music player that packs up to 1,000 CD-quality songs into an ultra-portable, 6.5-ounce design that fits in your pocket. iPod combines a major advance in portable music device design with Apple's legendary ease of use and Auto-Sync, which automatically downloads all your iTunes™ songs and playlists into your iPod, and keeps them up to date whenever you plug your iPod into your Mac®.

"With iPod, Apple has invented a whole new category of digital music player that lets you put your entire music collection in your pocket and listen to it wherever you go," said Steve Jobs, Apple's CEO. "With iPod, listening to music will never be the same again."[24]

The more common approach among technology companies at the time was to focus on technical specs. Apple chose to speak in consumer-benefit terms. "Putting 1,000 songs in your pocket" is selling the hole and not the drill.

Tip 3: Construct a Benefit Hierarchy.

Benefit laddering is a common way to uncover deep consumer insight, linking product attributes and benefits sought. When properly

constructed, a benefit hierarchy organizes thinking and signals identity and innovation opportunities.

A benefit hierarchy breaks down a particular product or category
into three components—product attributes, rational benefits, and
emotional benefits—with one "laddering up" to the next. In other
words, ask "Why?" three times.

The completed hierarchy shows—on one page—potential linkages
and gaps in creating and capturing new demand spaces at the product,
category, or brand level. Figure 2.3 provides an example from the automotive industry, starting from the bottom and working up.

Hypothesized Automotive Benefit Hierarchy

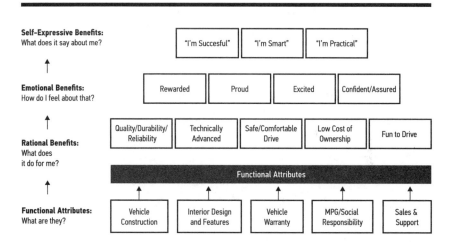

Figure 2.3

Here's the basic approach. First, begin with a broad definition of
the product or service category. Then, brainstorm the list of functional attributes that make up the current category, with a focus on
tangible things you can see, touch, taste, feel, or experience. Place
these on the bottom row.

From there, "ladder up" to the benefit areas to identify specific rational benefits associated with that attribute. The critical question here is *why. Why is this characteristic meaningful to me? What job does it do and why do I care?*

Next, ladder up yet again to define the emotional benefits. *Why is this benefit meaningful to me?* Some benefits will align with particular attributes, while others may require creating new linkages.

Finally, consider whether there are self-expressive benefits that consumers seek: *What does it say about me?*

Benefit hierarchies work across every industry—consumer goods and services, retail, technology, health-care products and services, financial services, insurance, and so on.

One key point regarding higher-order benefits: While it's useful to understand higher-order emotional linkages, don't necessarily focus at the top level. Understanding customer psyche can provide deep insight, but it may be too far removed to inform identity or innovation efforts.

Which benefits to focus on, including how high up on the ladder, depends on the category and the level of customer involvement, both rationally and emotionally.

MINI CASE EXAMPLE

Cardiac surgeons tend to be rational and precise in their language. We were hired by a medical device manufacturer to determine how best to market a breakthrough surgical therapy that recently received regulatory approval. Our work uncovered an important dynamic between the benefits and words "patient safety" and "ease of use."

Safety for physicians is the higher-order benefit, though many don't readily talk about it, as it introduces a potential negative—that something might be unsafe. Instead, they prefer language that touts ease of use. Surgeons then infer the device is safer. This learning helped finalize product positioning and marketing communications for launch.

A benefit hierarchy maps opportunities for uncovering and creating value. As a marketer, which benefits should you choose to deliver? What combinations of value are the most meaningful? In later chapters, we'll revisit the benefit hierarchy in the context of strategic growth areas, core offering, and positioning development.

Tip 4: Classify Benefits by Type.

Customers derive value from benefits. Typically, the more benefits a product delivers, the better. However, not all benefits are equal. In considering multiple benefits, think about the role each might play in a broader portfolio, as follows.

Ante benefits include the most essential benefits a brand, product, or service offers. These are "table stakes" that need to be delivered: Fast food needs to be fast. A convenience store should be convenient. Insurance companies should protect things. Prescription medications need to work. Once ante benefits are delivered, you can layer on other benefits to broaden value.

Driver benefits provide distinctiveness. Here, benefits extend beyond antes to drive differentiation and purchase. After delivering speedy service, a fast-food company might emphasize a fresher product. A financial services company might layer on personal relationship services. A prescription drug manufacturer might offer an extended-release form.

Reassurance benefits provide an emotional connection with the brand. These benefits are often best communicated implicitly rather than explicitly. Telling a customer to *feel* a certain way because of using a brand can be off-putting. Instead, deliver reassurance benefits through product quality cues and communication tone and manner.

In chapter 4, we introduce the concept of a value proposition. Each benefit can play a role on its own or combine with other value elements to create a broader proposition. The overall goal is to maximize the value through the most-desired combination of value elements.

Tip 5: Envision the Future State, Then Write It Down!

It may be a corporate cliché, but there's merit to hockey great Wayne Gretzky's quote, "Skate to where the puck is going, not where it has been." Be forward-thinking in uncovering opportunities. Said another way, don't look back, you're not going that way!

No one can predict the future, but with the right techniques, you can gather insight into potential new opportunities. Replacing the "rearview mirror" with a "windshield" view requires projective techniques to envision an optimal future state. Here's a useful approach.

PROJECTIVE TOOL TO BEGIN WITH THE END IN SIGHT

One way we get clients to begin with the end in sight is through a projective technique we refer to as "The Wall Street Journal Exercise."

The idea is to force team members to envision the future state very early in the project. Here are the prompts:

- Pick a date at a relevant point in time, say five years from today. Write the date at the top of a blank sheet of paper.

- Next, spend a few minutes thinking about where you'd like the organization to be five years from now. The future state should be aspirational, but also achievable, within the realm of possibility. Avoid blue-sky brainstorming and focus instead on a plausible stretch goal.

- Now, write the headline of a WSJ article capturing the essence of the future state. Like any good headline, it should encapsulate the main idea and leave the reader wanting to know more.

- Next, write a paragraph that describes the situation from two perspectives. Where are you today (the end state), and how did you get there (from the current state)? Fill in the how and the five W's: who, what, when, where, and why.

Read the article aloud and discuss it as a group. What's the headline? What happened? Why was it a success?

End-in-sight concepting is a great way to check internal alignment and identify strategy gaps to fill. Concepts can take a variety of forms, including verbal and visual descriptions to bring the idea to life. The key is to make them tangible and seek feedback to improve the ideas.

At Amazon, meetings to present ideas don't start with PowerPoint slides but with narratively structured memos. Jeff Bezos asks team members to submit six-page memos, which are then read—in silence—by meeting attendees.[25]

By having to write it all down—as opposed to dashing off quick bullet points or preparing PowerPoint slides—authors are forced to think through tough questions and formulate clear, persuasive replies, all while reasoning through the structure and logic.

Tip 6: Use Whiteboard Concepts and Strawman Proposals to Experiment and Learn.

Whiteboard Concepts and *strawman proposals* are two upstream marketing tools used to express ideas in draft form, to get feedback, and to iteratively optimize. The initial thoughts are not intended as the final answer, but rather as tools to get to the answer—the essence of create, test, and learn.

Whiteboard Concepts express new business and communication ideas as a starting point of the creative process. Write the concepts in the voice of end customers, including a benefit-based headline and a few lines of copy. Initially, the concepts are very crude—words on a blank page or computer screen, hence the phrase "whiteboard." Concepts are then exposed internally, and to customers, so that the ideas can be shaped and vetted over time, moving to increasingly better, next-level versions.

CREATING BENEFIT-BASED CONCEPTS

Here's a sample outline for preparing concept statements:

Create a headline that describes the core idea and benefit delivered. The shorter the better, as it will force you to be single-minded.

Describe the customer insight in one sentence. This is often the problem facing your customers. You want them nodding in agreement.

Explain your plan to help them, including one or two sentences that describe the product and corresponding benefits. The product solution should flow from the customer insight.

End by reinforcing the desired end state. Describe the ideal end-insight, through the eyes of the customer.

Concepts can be as short as a couple of sentences and as long as a page or two. The key is to focus on customer benefits and use language they can relate to. Clarify your message so customers engage.

Strawman proposals serve a similar role, though are used mainly for *internal purposes* to debate, pick apart, and improve draft ideas. A strawman is an initial draft proposal designed to generate discussion and provoke the creation of new and better alternatives.

Strawman business proposals can take many forms—a new business model canvas, a new business pitch deck, customer demand framework, and alternative brand architecture models. Presenting an idea as a first step is an invitation to knock it down and rebuild it better. Stamp "STRAWMAN" on the cover sheet and seek input. You're not selling the idea. You're looking to engage the team to improve upon it.

The dialogue and debate that accompany concepts and strawman proposals provide valuable insight to shape the final solution. These tools can literally get people on the same page in focusing on optimal solutions.

Tip 7: Establish an Insights Engine and Always Be Listening.

Every market is dynamic as customer needs evolve, new competitors enter, and the environment changes. And the rate of change is accelerating. Companies need to continually track and monitor marketplace needs through social listening, tracking studies, and other market research methods.

Here are just a few ways the profile companies obtain insights:

- Nike involves professional athletes in product development, along with employing a wide range of scientific disciplines including biomechanics, physiology, biomedical engineering, mechanical engineering, physics, and kinesiology.

- Starbucks uses crowdsourcing to improve customer satisfaction and innovation, allowing customers to submit ideas for new products on its company website.

- Disney uses virtual reality, augmented reality, and artificial intelligence to reimagine, design, and prototype how people experience entertainment using emerging technologies.

- Google's algorithms continuously build on its customers' collective intelligence so that Google repeatedly learns from—and about—its users.

- Amazon breaks down its business in formulaic terms, then captures metrics in real time to improve the customer experience.

While the methods vary, what's essential is systematically obtaining insight and infusing it with action to unlock growth.

USING SITUATION-COMPLICATION-RESOLUTION TO STRUCTURE PROBLEM SOLVING AND OBTAIN INSIGHT

Situation-complication-resolution, also known as SCR, is a problem-solving framework used by storytellers and consultants to structure thinking and gather insights.

EquiBrand uses SCR to categorize business issues and relay findings on client engagements. There are three parts.

1. **Situation** confirms the current state, in bullet point fashion. Start by telling your audience what they already know to put them at ease.

2. **Complication** identifies factors that are negatively impacting the situation. Describe the tension and underlying reasons it exists.

3. **Resolution** identifies the actions required to solve for the complications. What needs to happen to address the issues identified?

Examples of SCR are seen throughout this book, including some chapter 1 arguments, paraphrased here:

- **Situation:** Many business leaders see their playing field as fixed, and overemphasize downstream marketing. A downstream focus is necessary, but not sufficient.

- **Complication:** Upstream marketing is a proven way to grow, though it lacks familiarity, understanding, and practical instruction. It takes time, can be difficult to do, and may be hard to measure.

- **Resolution:** The upstream marketing framework provides a structured way to enact the principles of insight, identity, and innovation and six corresponding practices to answer four key strategy questions.

Consider using SCR any time you need to confirm issues, and craft an argument or proposition. It's a simple construct to create and easy for audiences to understand. For more information, see *The Pyramid Principle: Logic in Writing and Thinking* by Barbara Minto, a former McKinsey & Company consultant.

Insight is a required input to strategy development, and needs to clear a high hurdle: it must be deep, proprietary, forward-looking, and actionable. Maniacally focusing on the end customer promotes an outside-in perspective, which in turn leads to internal clarity and customer-centricity. From there, create a customer framework and confirm strategic growth opportunity areas, as in the topics described next.

QUESTIONS TO CONSIDER

1. What do you know about your important customers that your competitors don't know?

2. Have you structured insight gathering to obtain critical where-to-play and how-to-win perspectives?

3. How would you define the benefit hierarchy for the category in which you compete?

4. Are you using concept iteration to get people on the same page strategically?

CHAPTER 3

DEFINE YOUR PURPOSE— TO WHOM? FOR WHAT?

"Discovery consists of looking at the same thing as
everyone else and seeing something different."

—Albert Szent-Györgyi, *biochemist and Nobel Prize winner*

"Market segmentation is a natural result of the vast
differences among people."

—Donald A. Norman, *director of The Design Lab at
University of California, San Diego*

"If you're not thinking about target segments, you're not thinking."

—Theodore Levitt, *professor, Harvard Business School*

FROM A SINGLE STORE IN 1971 to over 30,000 global locations
today, Starbucks built its business on a core purpose and deep insight
into the coffee experience—that for coffee lovers, a cup of coffee is
much more than a hot morning drink made from roasted beans.

A cup of coffee, especially a Starbucks cup, is about the smell,
taste, sights, and sounds associated with a favorite beverage to start
the day. Sure, it's coffee, but it's also grabbing breakfast while checking
email. It's meeting with a family member, friend, or work colleague

throughout the day. It's having a comfortable "third place" (outside of home and work) to socialize and get stuff done.

Starbucks delivers a carefully choreographed customer experience supported by its mission: "To inspire and nurture the human spirit— one person, one cup, and one neighborhood at a time."[26]

Google was founded with a clear purpose: "Organize the world's information and make it universally accessible and usable."

When the company was just a few years old, the founders developed a list of "Ten things we know to be true." The list expounds upon the mission, with the number one priority to "Focus on the user and all else will follow."

As former Google CEO and Alphabet Chairman Eric Schmidt noted, Google's purpose directly influences the way it operates: "Google was founded to get information to everybody. A by-product of that strategy is that we invented an advertising business which has provided great economics that allows us to build the servers, hire the employees, create value."[27] From its company mission to customer value creation, Google is in alignment.

In the early 1970s, Southwest Airline's founders Herb Kelleher and Rollin King drew on a napkin the insight and idea that would revolutionize the airline industry.[28]

While other airlines targeted business customers and longer flights using a hub-and-spoke model, Southwest pursued another flyer segment through its point-to-point approach. It provided frequent, low-cost airline service in busy markets with shorter distances, with the first flights between Dallas, Houston, and San Antonio. Southwest's initial insight? Target the consumers who drive most of the time instead of flying, with frequent, no-frills service at the lowest possible cost.

Southwest links customer insight with founder Herb Kelleher's belief that if you put people first, the rest will follow. Kelleher said, "I tell my employees that we're in the service business, and it's incidental that we fly airplanes."[29] Southwest's purpose is to "Connect people to what's important in their lives through friendly, reliable, and low-cost air travel."[30] Southwest built a leading airline based on customer clarity, operational excellence, and a legendary corporate culture.

Amazon didn't set out to be in many of its current businesses when Jeff Bezos launched the company out of his garage in 1994. It did, though, set out to become the most customer-driven business, as reflected in its vision statement: "Our vision is to be earth's most customer-centric company; to build a place where people can come to find and discover anything they might want to buy online."[31]

Bezos is clear about where to look for business direction—the end customer. "If you're competitor-focused, you have to wait until there is a competitor doing something. Being customer-focused allows you to be more pioneering."[32]

Nike's purpose is "to unite the world through sport to create a healthy planet, active communities, and an equal playing field for all."[33] It may sound like a lofty goal for an athletic shoes and apparel company, but it speaks to why the company exists and aligns with their target consumers' aspirations.

Nike's early insight? "You can't explain much in sixty seconds, but when you show Michael Jordan, you don't have to. It's that simple," said Phil Knight, Nike CEO, describing the importance of consumer clarity and emotion in new product and brand development. Nike knows athletic performance is highly aspirational and uses athletes who embody the brand to make a consumer connection. Knight attributed Nike's early success to a mindset shift, recognizing the importance of building a strong emotional connection with the consumer. "We used to think that everything started in the lab. Now we realize that everything spins off the consumer."[34]

Steve Job's original mission for Apple: "To make a contribution to the world by making tools for the mind that advance humankind." Jobs also spoke about the importance of insight and simplicity. "That's been one of my mantras—focus and simplicity. Simple can be harder than complex: You have to work hard to get your thinking clean to make it simple. But it's worth it in the end because once you get there, you can move mountains."[35]

Walt Disney described his company's mission as "To make people happy."[36] Walt believed if you can dream it, you can do it. "We keep moving forward, opening up new doors, and doing new things, because we're curious . . . and curiosity keeps leading us down new paths."[37] Strong on curiosity and insight, Disney's success is moving beyond dreams to make them realities.

BEGIN WITH WHY

Starbucks nurtures the human spirit, one cup at a time. Google makes information universally accessible. Southwest connects people to what is important in their lives. Amazon strives to be the most customer-centric company in the world. Nike seeks to unite the world through sport. Apple simplifies technology. Disney makes people happy through magical, family entertainment.

These companies are all well known for their strong brands and innovative products. What drives their performance, though, is an aspirational purpose and a commitment to customer-centricity. They begin with *why*—using internal clarity to define their organization's aspiration—then leverage deep customer insight to chart new growth strategies.

The idea of beginning with why is described in Simon Sinek's famous TED talk and in his book *Start with Why: How Great Leaders Inspire Everyone to Take Action*. Says Sinek, "People don't buy what you do; they buy why you do it. And what you do simply proves what you believe." He continues, "Very few people or companies can clearly articulate *why* they do *what* they do. By *why* I mean your purpose, cause or belief—*Why* does your company exist? *Why* do you get out of bed every morning? And *why* should anyone care?"[38]

As the profile companies demonstrate, beginning with why inspires employees and helps solidify emotional connections with consumers and other stakeholders. The power of *why* is amplified when it links with to-whom and for-what insight.

TO WHOM? FOR WHAT?

When Steve Jobs returned to Apple in 1996, first as an advisor and then as interim CEO, one of the first things he did was refine the product strategy, beginning with the desktop computer portfolio.

After ten years of absence from the company he co-founded, he saw far too much complexity in how products were developed and marketed. He wanted to bring some focus, simplicity, and discipline to the product strategy.

During one meeting, he drew four boxes on a flipchart. Atop the two columns, he wrote "Consumer" and "Pro." He labeled the two rows "Desktop" and "Portable." The job, he said, was to make four great products, one for each quadrant (see figure 3.1).[39]

	Consumer	Pro
Desktop		
Portable		

Figure 3.1

This level of simplicity and focus is exactly what Apple needed then to deliver really strong products with specific targets in mind. Of course, Apple's product strategy is considerably more sophisticated today, but it continues to be defined by a clear, thoughtful approach to where-to-play decision making.

Interesting to note is where Apple decided *not* to focus. Apple has primarily stayed within the realm of hardware, software, and consumer products and services. Although they serve business-to-business customers, they leave much of that to Dell, HP, Lenovo, and other companies.

Southwest Airlines, by comparison, stays close to its core. Southwest focuses on low-cost airfare among business and vacation flyers and grows mainly by adding routes (organically and through acquisition). Sure, they've added credit cards and do a healthy business in freight, but mostly they're an airline serving airline customers. Also, the company offers a similar, relatively basic service experience to all its customers.

Starbucks maintains a fairly tight focus on its coffee and retail heritage. The company has pushed beyond morning coffee to a variety of beverage types (including tea and bottled drinks) and food items (bistro boxes, sandwiches, paninis, and salads).

They've also redesigned the in-store experience and invaded grocery stores and other outlets, so you can enjoy a latte while doing errands.

More recently, the company reallocated investments, selling off one of its tea brands and introducing the 15,000-square-foot Starbucks Reserve Roastery and Tasting Room to promote its rarest, small-batch coffees. Starbucks Reserve targets the most involved coffee connoisseur, in line with Starbucks' renewed commitment to its coffee heritage.

Each of these companies explicitly decides *to whom* its offerings should be targeted and *for what* particular need area. This to-whom, for-what mindset helps define the playing field. Some of the profile companies have a tight view of their market space; others take an expansive view. Either approach can be successful.

What they all employ is a purposefully defined strategy to approach specific customer segments with particular products, and *not* to pursue certain interests. This allows them to concentrate resources on the most promising areas.

ALIGNMENT IS THE KEY TO GROWTH

Defining your market space is a strategic choice regarding where to compete and where not to, across markets, customer groups, products, and channels. As shown in figure 3.2, it is an exercise in mapping customer segments (to whom?) and their needs (for what?).

This construct informs strategic growth areas and helps sharpen alignment with marketplace requirements. Having a clear strategy and plan for choosing the right businesses to invest in is paramount to upstream marketing.

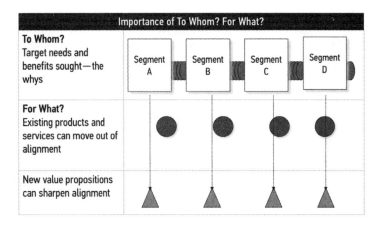

Figure 3.2

Growth Strategy Frameworks

In determining where to focus business growth, consider a few levels of strategic decision making and corresponding frameworks.

Level 1 regards whether to pursue "closer in" or "further out" opportunities. Should your focus be on the core business, adjacent areas, or diversification?

Level 2 uses traditional market segmentation methods—geographic, demographic, behavioral and attitudinal—to group customers.

Level 3, the domain of upstream marketing, directs where to focus precisely—which customers, needs, and offerings—drawing on a proprietary customer demand framework. The three levels are described in figure 3.3.

Three Growth Strategy Frameworks

Level 1

Growth Strategy 2 x 2 Matrix
Establishes four broad growth strategies, considering new and existing markets, and new and existing products

Level 2

Conventional Market Segmentations
Uses standard segmentation approaches—geographic, demographic, behavioral, and attitudinal—to group customers

Level 3

Customer Demand Framework
Uses proprietary insight to precisely inform to-whom, for-what and corresponding strategic opportunity areas

Figure 3.3

LEVEL 1—GROWTH STRATEGY MATRIX

At the base level, there are four classic growth strategies a company can pursue, hinging on whether markets are new or established and whether the company chooses to fill needs through existing or new products. Figure 3.4, derived from the Ansoff Matrix,[40] illustrates.

Growth Strategy 2 x 2 Matrix

		Markets	
		Existing	New
Products	**New**	Product Development	Diversification
	Existing	Market Penetration (Downstream Marketing)	Market Development

Figure 3.4

Let's use Amazon as an example of the Level 1 framework. Over time, Amazon has expanded well beyond its initial business to adjacent and diversified areas. Here's how.

FOUR PRIMARY GROWTH STRATEGIES

Market Penetration involves increasing market share by filling the needs of existing markets with existing products. Launched as "Earth's biggest bookstore," Amazon spent its early days establishing itself as an online alternative to traditional book retailers by expanding book titles and making consumers comfortable with a new way of shopping. The company focused on downstream marketing, pulling classic marketing levers: creating awareness, tweaking the product, and improving communication. Had Amazon decided to fixate here, it would not be nearly the company it is today.

Product Development involves identifying additional needs among existing customers and then satisfying these needs through new offerings. Even before Jeff Bezos started Amazon, he drew up a list of twenty potential products he would sell on the Internet, including software, CDs, and books. Once Amazon established its core infrastructure with books, other

continued

product categories were sold online. Amazon has also created its own products and services, including Kindle, Fire, Echo, and original content. These provide existing customers with new ways to experience content and other offerings.

Market Development entails finding new markets for existing products through segmentation and targeted communication. Just as Amazon disrupted traditional bookselling, it did the same with textbooks. Recognizing the high cost of textbooks and students' constrained budgets, Amazon introduced new programs to develop this market, including renting, selling, and repurchasing schoolbooks.

Diversification involves attacking new markets with new offerings at the same time. Within books, for example, Amazon established Kindle Direct Publishing (KDP), directly targeting authors to both publish and promote their books. Initial draft copies of *Upstream Marketing*, for example, bypassed traditional publishing and used KDP instead. While diversification has the highest upside, it's also the riskiest strategy. The more a company moves from its comfort zone, the greater the uncertainty. However, diversification can lead to substantial new revenue if successful.

The advantage of the first-level growth matrix is that it's simple and works. The 2 x 2 framework describes broad, strategic choices to focus marketing. However, while the model is strategically and managerially helpful, it's too far removed from end customers to provide rich insight and inspire growth.

Also, many companies are trapped in the lower-left, downstream quadrant: How do we sell more of the same stuff to the same people? To expand their thinking and uncover market-based opportunities, next-level customer insight is needed.

LEVEL 2—CONVENTIONAL MARKET SEGMENTATIONS

Second-level decision frameworks include commonly used methods of customer segmentation, including geographic, demographic, behavioral, and attitudinal/needs-based. These are described here using The Walt Disney Company examples.

CONVENTIONAL SEGMENTATION APPROACHES[41]

Geographic segmentation is used when language, cultural, ethnicity, and other factors are present. Beginning with Disneyland Resort in California and Walt Disney World Resort in Florida, Disney Parks has expanded to include Paris, Tokyo, Hong Kong, and Shanghai. Disney delivers a consistent value proposition across all geographies, slightly modified to reflect local audiences.

Demographic segmentation uses age, income, household makeup, and life stage to define segments. Disney has created four hotels and resorts tiers—Value, Moderate, Deluxe, and Disney Vacation Club Villas—that appeal to different demographic targets. The Grand Floridian, its flagship resort, commands room rates of over $1,000 per night. This compares with Value rates of $100 to $200. Disney offers a similar magical experience—the same attractions, characters, and fun factor—though at different value levels for different demographics.

Behavioral segmentation divides a market by shopping and buying behaviors. Disney employs behavioral segmentation in determining marketing and pricing strategies for its theme park tickets. It uses sophisticated data analytics to carefully manage ticket pricing to encourage extended resort stays and provides a series of annual passports that combine valuable discounts, offers, and special events.

Attitudinal segmentation (also called psychographic segmentation) separates customers based on attitudes, motivations, and needs. Disney conducts market research with its highly involved attitudinal group, commonly referred to as "Disneyphiles." This group visits parks multiple times a year and eats, sleeps, and breathes anything Disney. Gaining deep insight into Disney's most loyal segment benefits the entire organization.

Many companies rely on demographics and firmographics (for business customers) for growth planning, as these groups are easier to find and measure. Proponents of these methods argue, "If you can't measure it, you can't manage it."

While these approaches work for certain downstream activities, they are ill-suited when insight into consumer attitudes, motivations, and needs is vital. Remember, just because "the light is better there" doesn't mean it's the place to look.

MINI CASE EXAMPLE

Segmenting customers by needs and attitudes provides richer, more meaningful insight than demographic measures like age and income. We were hired by a biopharmaceutical company to help strategically market their FDA-approved inhalable insulin product for patients with diabetes.

Through qualitative and quantitative segmentation research, we identified two primary factors in separating patients with diabetes into clustered preferences. First, patients' fear and acceptance of needle injections. Second, patients' understanding and diligence in how they managed their diabetes—did they comply with or ignore doctors' orders in how they managed their condition?

Based on this customer clarity, we were able to segment and then obtain rich insight into patient motivations. It turns out, patient attitudes toward needles, self-administration, and compliance are much more meaningful than gender, age, and income.

LEVEL 3—PROPRIETARY CUSTOMER DEMAND FRAMEWORK

A third-level framework articulates customer segments and their attitudes, needs, and behaviors, and begins to identify growth opportunity areas to pursue, including market sizing.

A Level 3 framework differs from Levels 1 and 2 as it is *proprietary*, emphasizes *new market spaces*, provides *alignment* of products with the marketplace, and serves as a *common platform* shared within the organization.

The framework itself consists of three interrelated elements—customer segments, potential needs, and strategic opportunity areas—as shown in figure 3.5.

Think about a customer demand framework as a strategic chessboard: Across the top, align customer groups your organization could potentially serve. Then, on the left, group market-based opportunities: What needs do customers have? What benefits are they seeking? What jobs need to be done? Any areas of unmet need represent unoccupied white space opportunities. Like a master chess player, this allows a company to strategically identify, plan for, and move into new demand spaces, making competition irrelevant.

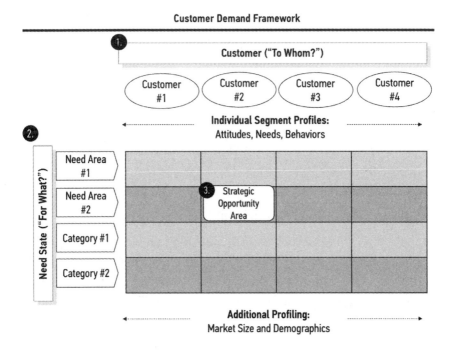

Figure 3.5

The most useful Level 3 frameworks combine standard segmentation methods with proprietary market insight. Customer attitudes, behaviors, and demographics are *combined* into a composite sketch of opportunities. The framework then informs value proposition creation, brand positioning, customer experience, and product portfolio development.

To be clear, a Level 3 framework is *not* about dividing up existing–and often shrinking–market opportunities. A Level 3 framework is designed to uncover and size new market spaces to capture unmet demand. Find the deep that unites, by aggregating demand across customers and non-customers to maximize brand and market opportunities.

Developing a Level 3 customer demand framework

There are a variety of ways to create customer management frameworks, ranging from simple, qualitatively developed frameworks to highly sophisticated, quantitatively based methods.

Level 3 frameworks often begin as a hypothetical sketch on a whiteboard and are then validated through the computational power of statistical modeling and data analytics. To illustrate:

Picture a large room, like an auditorium, filled with 100 potential consumers of your category. Now, split the 100 consumers into five to seven smaller breakout rooms, based on how they buy products and services, including their attitudes, needs, and behaviors—not based on demographics.

By way of example, consider 100 potential consumers within the automotive insurance category. One customer group may value a personal, neighborly association with their insurance agent. Another may prefer to handle the insurance experience entirely online—with no human interaction. Perhaps a third segment looks for the absolute lowest cost provider, and a fourth group is made up of people who are concerned they might not qualify for coverage due to poor driving records.

After the segments are identified, build out the Level 3 framework and fully profile individual customer groups, including their attitudes, motivations, and benefits sought. Use insight from actual customer interactions and available research to populate the framework and create segment profiles. Paint a picture of each consumer group. Use stock photos, illustrations, and other tools to bring the segments to life visually—Who are they? What defines them? What are their needs? How do they buy?

Quantitative surveys can then be used to numerically validate and size opportunities. Finding patterns in actual buying behavior among current and potential customers can indicate where the largest sources of demand, revenue and profit may lie. Survey questions can be worded as "I wish" statements to identify growth areas, including uncontested white space opportunities (where no other competitor has a strong presence).

BE CAREFUL WITH BUYER PERSONAS

Personas are fictional representations of your target customers "brought to life" through a composite sketch. They provide a mental model of end customers: who they are, what motivates them, and what causes them to engage—or not engage—with your brand.

Because it's so valuable to see your business through your customers' eyes, be sure these personas reflect actual views in the marketplace, ideally confirmed through quantitative segmentation.

The risk of qualitatively based personas is that they can be designed to reflect desired or imagined groups rather than actual consumers.

Personas should be fact-based and derived from the entire market—start with 100 consumers and divide from there. That way, you'll know whether you're pulling from an actual clustered choice instead of creating a persona that might relate to a diffused or imagined preference.

Ultimately, to-whom and for-what decision making will shape your entire business model and go-to-market approach, so plan and choose wisely.

Look for Clustered Preferences

The key to a robust to-whom, for-what level 3 framework is when clear, clustered preferences emerge across potential customer segments. To do this, use a demand- or needs-based rather than a competitor- or product-based view of the category. This makes it easy to uncover untapped market spaces, and align potential offerings with customer needs. In most cases, customers have clustered preferences like these shown in figure 3.6.

Impact of Clustered Preferences on Segmentation

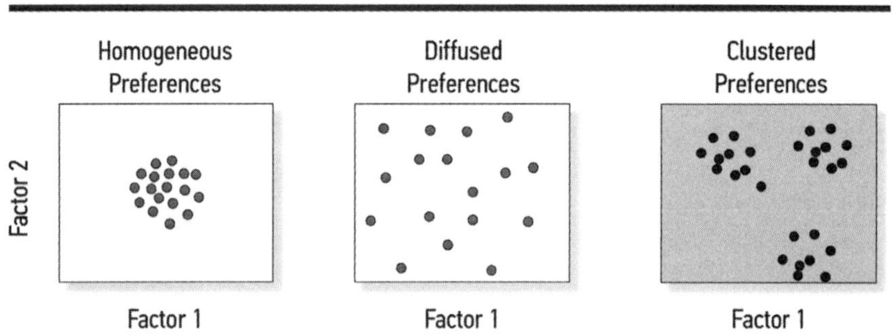

Figure 3.6

There are several advantages to uncovering and delivering on clustered preferences. First, customer clarity helps precisely define what makes one group tick versus others. New products can be laser-focused, improving business success rates. Second, resources can be targeted rather than trying to be all things to all people. Most organizations are resource-constrained and segmentation lets them "place their bets," focusing rather than diffusing resources. Finally, a needs- or attitudinal-based view helps identify unmet needs and tap uncontested upstream opportunities.

After creating the customer framework, it's time to prioritize targets and immerse yourself in the target customer experience.

TARGET MARKETING

Targeting is one of the most important, though often overlooked, components to marketing success. Many business leaders are reluctant to select a target, fearing that excluding certain groups will eliminate potential sources of volume. As a result, they define the market too broadly or try to serve all customers equally. They end up offering an average product that appeals to no one.

Other executives look for finer, more precise segmentations, and in doing so, end up slicing the market too narrowly and end up chasing smaller demand.

More adept marketers know that balanced targeting results in a stronger brand—the more focused the target, the deeper the understanding, the better equipped you are to deliver on strategic opportunity areas for growth.

MINI CASE EXAMPLE

"Anybody with money." That was the unfortunate answer from the SVP of sales of a global financial services company. We had asked him who he thought the target should be for a new product we were helping his company develop. It was a poor targeting choice. At some level, nearly *everyone* has money. Creating an undifferentiated offering, marketing it to everyone, and hoping someone buys it is inefficient. A shotgun approach to marketing is bound to fail. Fuzzy targets don't get hit.

Marketing Target vs. Consumption Market

Best practice marketers understand the distinction between (1) a focused "target market" (the center of the bull's-eye) and (2) the broader "consumption market" that falls outside of the core target, but often finds the offering appealing. "Speak to the target, but let others listen" distills target marketing down to actionable insight (see figure 3.7).

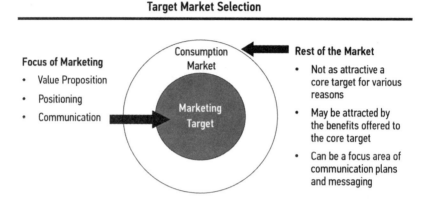

Target Market Selection

Focus of Marketing
- Value Proposition
- Positioning
- Communication

Consumption Market

Marketing Target

Rest of the Market
- Not as attractive a core target for various reasons
- May be attracted by the benefits offered to the core target
- Can be a focus area of communication plans and messaging

Speak to the target, but let others listen

Figure 3.7

The Targeting Paradox

Target selection presents an interesting paradox. Often, the tighter the target definition, the broader the appeal among the consumption market. In other words, the smaller the center circle in figure 3.7 (the marketing target), the larger the outer circle (the consumption group). Laser-focused brands attract broader consumer groups, which results in greater sales from both current and potential new customers. Here are a few examples.

TARGETING AT NIKE

Nike targets athletes, broadly defined, as reflected in its mission statement. Within this broader market, the center of the bull's-eye is actually *performance athletes*. Targeting true athletes provides an aspirational element to the brand and also impacts how Nike operates.

For example, Nike involves world-class athletes in its product development efforts, creating optimal shoes and apparel for their use. A case in point is Nike's development and launch of the Vaporfly Elite Flyprint 3D. Only runners who could run a marathon in three hours or less qualified to purchase these shoes, initially made available in limited quantities and priced at over $600 per pair.

Of course, Nike sells a lot of shoes to non-athletes, representing the much broader consumption target. Extending out from the core are weekend warriors and further out, less involved targets, who, while not particularly athletic, aspire to "be like Mike."

Making performance athletes the bull's-eye brings clarity and commitment to the organization. Phil Knight said, "We wanted Nike to be the world's best sports and fitness company. Once you say that, you have a focus. You don't end up making wing tips or sponsoring the next Rolling Stones world tour."[42]

Notably, Nike sold off its non-athletic Cole Haan shoe division in 2012 and divested other assets to focus its efforts and better align with its mission.

TARGETING AT APPLE

Apple uses a similar approach in targeting involved consumers to penetrate new markets and categories. Apple designs its products for creative consumers, and its core marketing target is hardcore Apple loyalists—folks who preorder products online or grab them the first day they're available in-store.

Even before launch, Apple gets expert bloggers, thought leaders, and influencers on board to create buzz. Through PR, viral marketing, and word-of-mouth, broader groups begin to purchase the product, and sales skyrocket. Apple maintains a tight marketing target, with an eye toward the broader consumption market.

Sure, Apple has an extensive, growing business with schools, corporations, and other enterprises. Its core marketing target, though, remains the consumer. Steve Jobs said, "Our DNA is as a consumer company—for that individual customer who's voting thumbs up or thumbs down. That's who we think about."[43]

The Apple loyalist consumer who loves her MacBook, iPad, and iPhone? She may also serve as the purchasing director for a Fortune 500 company at her day job. In targeting consumer loyalists, Apple also attracts business users—the targeting paradox at work.

TARGETING ACROSS INDUSTRIES

The targeting paradox is common across industries. Pharmaceutical companies often target thought leaders and specialty physicians to endorse their brand's effectiveness with primary care physicians and pharmacists, who are considered the consumption market.

Software companies often prioritize power users in product development, even though the bulk of product sales come from casual users. Similarly, auto manufacturers often put coveted road-and-track enthusiasts at the center of their bull's-eye instead of the average driver.

More involved consumers tend to be more demanding, setting higher performance standards and rewarding companies that meet them with greater brand loyalty and word-of-mouth marketing. Targeting aspirational groups stimulates interest and demand from broader consumption groups.

Target Selection Criteria

Selecting targets is an issue of prioritization—while you don't want to exclude anyone from purchasing, a focused target results in a stronger value proposition, brand positioning, and go-to-market plan. Four standard target evaluation criteria include:

- **Segment size:** Is the segment sufficiently large including non-customer prospects?

- **Segment growth:** Is the segment growing and on-trend with where the market is heading?

- **Brand fit:** Does the target customer align with our company purpose, mission, vision, goals and brand?

- **Segment attractiveness:** Can we win—do the segment's needs match our ability to deliver?

It's often easier to determine first who *not* to target, which becomes a process of elimination and can help narrow your choices.

WHO *NOT* TO TARGET

In marketing an offering, rather than consider, "Who should we target?" ask, "Who *shouldn't* we target?" It's sometimes easier to whittle down targets than to take a bottom-up approach. The result is the same. It's just another way to get to the answer.

Posing the question this way forces discipline in making trade-offs. In the inhalable insulin mini case example, we decided to *not* target noncompliant patients, recognizing it would be difficult to win with this segment.

In other categories, we've deemphasized price-driven consumers who chase deals and are unlikely to demonstrate brand loyalty.

Defining the bull's-eye and the segments falling outside the center helps determine which groups will receive focused expenditures and investments.

In summary, one of the root causes of poor business performance is the failure to select a core marketing target. Companies that try to be all things to all people often do not stand for any one thing, resulting in diluted marketing. The inability to define and select a clear target, then, often results in a murky brand positioning or failed new product launch.

In the end, making hard targeting decisions helps increase your chances of market success. As we've seen with the targeting paradox, selecting a focused marketing target does not restrict business potential. It often means the opposite.

STRATEGIC OPPORTUNITY AREAS

The intersection of the to-whom, for-what framework results in strategic opportunity areas (SOAs)—or fishing ponds from our chapter 1 analogy. Think of SOAs as significant, attractive "innovation buckets" in which to look for profitable growth. They often represent pockets of unmet customer demand, to be filled through new products, new services, geographic expansions, brand extensions, new channels, acquisitions, improved market communication, and internal initiatives.

Most companies intuitively think about strategic opportunities, but not in an organized way. Often, demand spaces reside in the minds of business leaders and don't move beyond that stage. The key is to write them down using a consistent format. This makes the areas tangible so that they can be evaluated and prioritized. Figure 3.8 offers a sample SOA template.

Potential sources of growth stem from areas already talked about—customer, marketplace, and technical insight. These inputs add context and texture for the SOA written description.

In filling out the template, describe the target customer situation, their needs, and benefits sought. Later, you'll use concept iteration to develop potential solutions.

Strategic Opportunity Area Development

- Potential growth sources
  - ✓ Unmet customer needs
  - ✓ Market trends
  - ✓ Portfolio gaps
  - ✓ Technological innovation
  - ✓ Competitive opportunities
  - ✓ Supplier opportunities
  - ✓ Etc.

- Write them down in a consistent format so they can be evaluated and prioritized

Target Description

Customer Need

Consumer Insight

Benefit Provided

Opportunity Sizing

Figure 3.8

Here are broad, strategic opportunity areas from EquiBrand clients, using the how-might-we problem statement setup:

- For a luxury automotive manufacturer, how might we design a sales and service experience for the one-third of customers who prefer to skip the dealer experience entirely?

- For a traditional automotive insurance company, how might we sell new financial products and services, including retirement planning, investment management, and trust services, to existing insurance clients?

- For a food manufacturer of prepackaged mixes, how might we deliver a Starbucks or specialty-bakery dessert experience at home?

- For a retail bank, how might we attract consumer segments across multiple cultures and backgrounds through an improved customer experience?

- For a biopharmaceutical company, how might we improve patient compliance to promote better care and improved quality of life?

- For a manufacturer of backpacks, how might we penetrate the workplace with a new line of packs that combine the professionalism of a briefcase with the convenience of a traditional backpack?

- For a small kitchen appliance maker, how might we create a "driving idea" to increase cooking confidence through tips and recipes on Pinterest and other social platforms?

- For a public library, how might we transform the customer experience, recognizing the shift to remote learning, makerspace, and digital programming and away from physical books?

- For an enterprise software company, how might we create a direct-to-consumer vision, strategy, and investor pitch deck to secure funding and expand the business.

A strategy session or brainstorming session could yield many opportunity areas, often a dozen or more. That's too many for most companies to handle. Even Apple only works on a few projects at a time, choosing to concentrate its resources rather than diffusing them across hundreds of efforts. So, you'll need to narrow the list.

Prioritizing Strategic Opportunity Areas

There are numerous ways to screen growth areas, though the principles are the same. The impact-effort matrix is a great early way to assess and prioritize strategic opportunities at a high level using an investment mindset. In figure 3.9, consider impact to be the return, and effort to be the investment, with the end objective to maximize your return on investment.

Impact-Effort Matrix

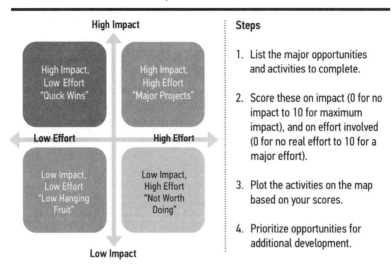

High Impact

Steps

High Impact,
Low Effort
"Quick Wins"

High Impact,
High Effort
"Major Projects"

Low Effort   **High Effort**

Low Impact,
Low Effort
"Low Hanging
Fruit"

Low Impact,
High Effort
"Not Worth
Doing"

Low Impact

1. List the major opportunities and activities to complete.

2. Score these on impact (0 for no impact to 10 for maximum impact), and on effort involved (0 for no real effort to 10 for a major effort).

3. Plot the activities on the map based on your scores.

4. Prioritize opportunities for additional development.

Figure 3.9

Use business judgement and experience initially to qualitatively assess potential. As ideas begin to take shape over time, screening will get more granular as you obtain customer insight and metrics to evaluate. See chapter 6 for more detail about what-would-have-to-be-true business screening across strategic, customer, financial, and operational areas.

Confirming Where to Play

Use the Level 3 customer framework to plot and manage your corporate growth strategy. Going back to the chessboard example, any point of intersection (the square for the chess piece) provides you with the opportunity to establish and define a strategic opportunity area.

Emerging companies might focus on one square, establishing and protecting their beachhead from competitors. Established companies may extend their business to encompass adjacent white space or unoccupied opportunities.

After identifying and prioritizing where to play opportunities, it's time to get smart on the market space and obsess about how to win with the marketing target. This involves placing bets on how best to aim value proposition and brand development efforts, as described in the next two chapters.

In the end, target insight and alignment are vital to growth. In practice, this means having a clear purpose and customer demand framework to understand segment needs and opportunities, then preparing targeted offerings to align with their needs.

MOVING FROM INSIGHT TO IDENTITY

"Five hundred dollars for a plane ticket and I can't even get a free snack!" The flight attendant just told the stranger sitting next to us that the airline no longer offered complimentary snacks. If he wanted food, he'd have to pay for it.

For the next half hour, the disgruntled customer talked about his frustrations with airline travel, including the "principle" of not getting a free bag of peanuts.

With nothing but time on our hands, we probed for deeper insight and learned he was a frequent flyer and preferred certain airlines, mainly based on customer service. He didn't like to travel, as it took him away from his family. For him, the free snack had emotional significance.

He spoke of being awarded ribbons at his grade school track meets. It was hard work, and he earned it. He likened the bag of snacks to a reward, a ribbon, for his travels.

He questioned the logic and cost savings of the airline's actions. At one point, he did a back-of-the-napkin calculation (after all, soft drinks were still free) about the airline's savings. He concluded, "It's like the old saying, accountants know the cost of everything but the value of nothing."

A couple of things to note from this example: First, how easy it is to obtain consumer insight, and yet how many companies ignore it. Many companies emphasize data, but lack insight. The emotional connection a frequent flyer has with a bag of snacks won't show up on a spreadsheet.

Second, how some companies make better use of insights in developing strong brands and driving innovation. Southwest Airlines, for example, still offers low fares and freebies—checked bags, free TV, no change fees—and has one of the highest profit margins in the industry.

Does Southwest have *better* insight or do a better job of using it in business operations? It turns out the answer is yes to both. Best-in-class companies are committed to gathering insight *and* applying it to improve marketing and business operations.

Principle 1 described the role of purpose and customer-centricity in identifying where-to-play opportunities. In Principle 2, we explore how to win by developing compelling value propositions and strong brands. We move from defining the playing field to fielding a winning team. We move from insight to identity.

QUESTIONS TO CONSIDER

1. *Why* does the organization do what it does? What is its purpose?

2. To whom—on which customer segment—should you target your growth efforts?

3. For what—which high-potential strategic opportunity areas should be targeted?

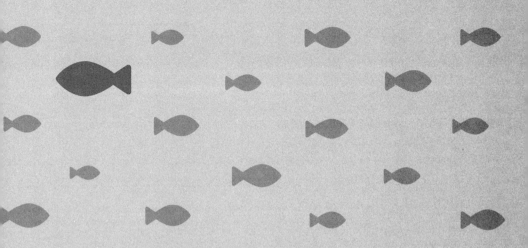

PRINCIPLE 2

Identity

IDENTITY

AMAZON, APPLE, GOOGLE, NIKE, SOUTHWEST, Starbucks, and Walt Disney.

What comes to mind when you think of these companies? What thoughts, feelings, and impressions do you have? How employees, customers, and investors see and experience a company or product *is* its identity. When done right, what the market sees is in alignment with how the company views itself.

The best companies create strong, winning identities, both with employees and customers. That identity then shapes how the company operates and distinguishes its brand from competitors. Product patents, technical know-how, and barriers to entry can be fleeting. A brand is one of the few things a company can own forever.

Our best practice research suggests three key steps to achieve a strong identity. First, as discussed in Principle 1, intentionally define what you want to become, including a deep and shared understanding of the customer and your organization's purpose.

Next, develop value propositions that embody that identity—at the corporate, business unit, and product level. As discussed in chapter 4, this requires identifying and aligning three things: prioritized customer needs, benefits delivered, and operational strategies and tactics.

Finally, build a strong brand that communicates the identity and value proposition internally and externally. A well-defined brand serves as a touchstone for strategic decision making, resonates with target audiences, and results in a distinctive brand identity. Chapter 5 lays out the four keys to brand management: brand positioning, brand-customer experience, brand architecture, and brand extension.

Identity, value proposition, and brand strategy are related concepts—each should inform, reflect, and reinforce the other, as shown in figure P2.1.

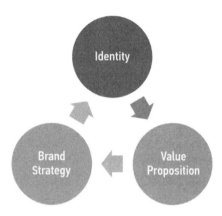

Figure P2.1

It's important to distinguish the upstream marketing principle of identity as separate from *corporate identity*, which is a business term associated with a company's logo or style guide.

Most companies have a logo and a distinct look and feel, but many lack a strong identity. The substance of a brand, like a person's character, is beneath the surface.

Leading companies succeed by obtaining deep customer insight, strategically placing bets on portfolio opportunities, and establishing and communicating a winning identity, value proposition, and positioning. The strongest brand identities are built upstream. Let's dive in.

CHAPTER 4

DESIGN AND ALIGN VALUE PROPOSITIONS

"The value of identity, of course, is that so often with it comes purpose."
—Richard Grant, *actor, screenwriter, and director*

"What you think you become, what you feel you attract,
what you imagine you create."
—Buddha

"Design is a funny word. Some people think design means how it looks.
But of course, if you dig deeper, it's really how it works."
—Steve Jobs, *co-founder, chairman, and CEO of Apple, Inc.*

PURPOSE. MISSION. VISION. VALUES. There is a confusing array of concepts and terms. Which is which, and how do they relate? A cynic might consider such topics corporate navel-gazing at the expense of taking action.

Still, it's hard to argue with the power these inputs hold in strategy development. As we'll see in chapter 7, each profile company, and virtually every Fortune 500 company, uses corporate statements to guide decision making, align actions, build the brand, and steer the corporate culture.

Howard Schultz of Starbucks connects the company's purpose, brand, and culture this way: "I think the structural issue, first and foremost in building a brand and maintaining that equity, is establishing trust and confidence with the two constituencies, which are your people and your customers. And it can't be like 90 percent of the time, it's got to be 100 percent of the time. 'This is who we are, this is what we stand for.' This goes back to core purpose and reason for being. It all ties back. The equity of the brand has to be a reflection of the culture of the company. It can't be something off to the side. It is not an adjacency. It has to be fully integrated, where everything kind of matches up."[44]

THE ROLE OF CORPORATE STATEMENTS

Mission, vision, and values—which we collectively refer to as *corporate statements*—work together to inform decisions and obtain internal alignment:

Direction	Role	Analogy
Mission	Explains the organization's core purpose and direction.	The heart of your business
Vision	Describes the ideal future state. What do you want to be when you grow up?	The eyes of your business
Values	Describes what the organization believes in and how it behaves.	The soul of your business

Ask, does the decision we're about to make—where to invest, what we offer, who we hire—fit with the company's mission, vision, and values? If so, proceed. If not, reconsider.

Corporate Statement Limitations

Though mission, vision, and value statements are important inputs, there are limitations.

These statements, especially when reduced to a few words or phrases, can be ambiguous. Employees may wonder how to put the business into action: We have a mission statement . . . now what?

These aspirational statements tend to be internal rather than customer-driven. They may *talk* about being customer-driven, but the statements themselves are often void of specific customer benefits.

Furthermore, mission, vision, and values tend to operate at the corporate level and may lack relevance at the division or product level. In a desire to unify the organization, these statements get watered down. They don't provide the specificity necessary for strategic decision making.

Finally, corporate statements don't drive revenue growth. Customers can buy *into* a company's values, but they cannot purchase the statements. They buy offerings—products, services, and other elements of value.

TWO CRITICAL IDENTITY ELEMENTS

While corporate statements are useful, two additional strategy elements are needed for upstream marketing—the value proposition, and the brand strategy. The next chart describes both, and we discuss each in order.

Direction	Role	Analogy
Value proposition	Determines which benefits to stand for and deliver on to align with target customer needs.	The arms and legs of your business
Brand strategy	Establishes the long-term plan for developing and delivering an aspirational brand identity.	The face of your business

The *value proposition* is the missing link that connects customer needs with the organization, which guides how-to-win efforts.

Value propositions put customer insight into relevant business operational terms, making it easier to make decisions and develop action plans. A value proposition (or core offering) is where value is both delivered to and extracted from customers in the form of revenues.

Unlike a mission or vision statement, value propositions focus explicitly on customer needs, delivering concrete products and services people buy. Though an organization has one vision, mission, or set of values, it can have multiple value propositions and brand positionings across products and services.

Let's explore value proposition next, then pick up with brand strategy and positioning in the next chapter.

VALUE PROPOSITION EXAMPLE

In our consulting work, we often use Amazon to introduce the concept of a value proposition. First, we describe the core framework, then ask client team members to recreate it on paper or a dry-erase board, filling in and revising details as they go (see figure 4.1).

As you'll see, since the propositions tend to be multidimensional, the framework extends beyond a single statement. Also, to make it actionable, the template links customer needs with brand benefits and operational strategies.

Finally, the framework foreshadows the power of upstream marketing integration. Column one relates to insight. Column two to identity—communicable brand benefits. The third column relates to innovation.

When well-constructed, one value proposition element snaps into another like a magnet. As we'll show, a multiplier effect then occurs as each upstream principle—insight, identity and innovation—informs and reflects the other.

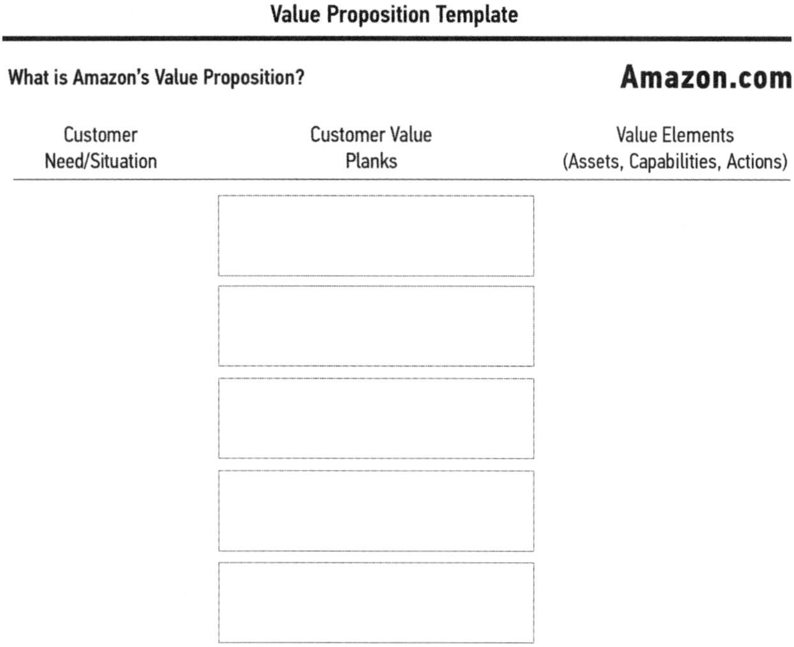

Value Proposition Template

What is Amazon's Value Proposition?   **Amazon.com**

Customer Need/Situation	Customer Value Planks	Value Elements (Assets, Capabilities, Actions)

Figure 4.1

These are the prompts:

- In the first column, under Customer Need/Situation, describe Amazon's typical customer and broad need areas. Who is at the center of the bull's-eye, and what do they value? Group the needs into the top half dozen or so. Complete the statement: I need

  _____.

- Next, under Customer Value Planks in the second column (also called brand benefit planks) describe the benefits associated with Amazon. What does Amazon stand for and what core benefits does it deliver in meeting customer needs?

- Then, under the last column, Value Elements, list and organize individual assets, capabilities, and actions associated with Amazon. Individual value elements contribute to and build out the value planks and might include product and service components, branded items, the online shopping experience, and other features. Across the organization, what is being done or could be done to deliver on the value planks? What are the reasons to believe?

- Revisit the summary template and improve it from two perspectives. First, moving from left to right, do the customer needs, benefit planks, and value elements align, so there is logic and order? Then, moving from top to bottom, are the key benefits that define Amazon captured?

Check and recheck the framework vertically and horizontally to determine other areas of value. Finally, present and discuss the draft framework with the group.

The result of the exercise? With surprising consistency, team members are able to describe Amazon's primary value set on one page. As massive as Amazon is, there is consistency in the brand's identity. Figure 4.2 shows an example developed from one workshop.

Value Proposition Development

Amazon Case example

Consumer Need/Situation	Value Planks	Value Elements (Assets, Capabilities, Action)
Convenient shopping experience	Any Time, Any Place Online Shopping	• 24/7/365 access, 1-Click ordering • Knows you, knows your preferences • Cross-channel capable (online, voice, in-person)
Variety and choice	Expansive Selection	• Widest product selection • Reviews and product information • Product suggestions
Speed and efficiency	Next Day, Same Day, Hourly Delivery	• One-day shipping, local deliveries • Logistics infrastructure • Low cost structure

Free shipping and easy returns	Amazon Prime (handled as sub-brand)	• With membership fee
		   – Free shipping
		   – Unlimited streaming of available movies
		   – Book borrowing from Kindle
		   – Etc.

Consolidated media purchases		

Source: EquiBrand Consulting analysis

Figure 4.2

Next, we probe and discuss Amazon. Which value planks are ante, driver, and reassurance benefits? How do customer needs sought and value planks relate?

Reading down the first column, the first three customer needs—convenient shopping experience, variety and choice, and speed and efficiency—are table stake requirements of most online shoppers. Amazon, though, has introduced differentiation through individual elements—1-Click purchasing, customer reviews, same-day shipping—to win with consumers.

The fourth and fifth planks, regarding Amazon Prime, emerged over time. Initially launched in 2005, Prime was Amazon's answer to customers' desire for free shipping, offering free two-day shipping for an initial $79 fee.

After a while, the Prime sub-brand evolved organically to include a host of other services, including consolidated media purchases and streaming music and video.

Amazon and Amazon Prime show how value stacks occur at different levels. Corporately, Amazon delivers certain benefits—convenience, choice, speed, and efficiency. Amazon Prime then taps into these corporate benefit associations, adding new value elements for customers seeking a subscription service.

Of course, Amazon has numerous other brands and businesses. Each has its own value proposition and may link with Amazon's core online retail business.

Across its entire portfolio, Amazon starts with the customer and then works backward to craft innovative value planks and propositions.

VALUE PROPOSITION FRAMEWORK

At the most basic level, a value proposition defines how to win by linking three things—customer needs, benefits sought, and assets and capabilities. When all three parts align, the organization creates and captures value. Let's take a closer look at each component in figure 4.3.

Value Proposition Framework

Customer Need/Situation	⟷ Value Planks ⟷	Value Elements (Assets, Capabilities, Action)
Deep insight into target customers' situation and needs	The set of benefit planks that fulfill customer needs	Products, services, programs, and operations to deliver the benefits customers seek

Figure 4.3

The customer need/situation describes the base-level needs of the target audience. What does your target customer desire? As described in Principle 1 on insight, you can obtain customer clarity through a variety of methods, including in-depth interviews, ethnographic studies, and data analytics.

Value planks, the middle column, define key benefits delivered to the target customer. These can be functional, emotional, self-expressive benefits, or expressed as jobs to be done.

The final column describes operational components used to deliver on customer needs and benefits sought. This consists of individual value elements—capabilities, competencies, and other assets the organization can provide.

Individual value elements combine to create value planks, which in turn form the total value proposition.

To unlock growth, a company can improve existing value

propositions or create entirely new ones. In some cases, value can be created by combining *existing* value elements in *new* ways. Consider for example how Amazon, Amazon Prime, and Whole Foods combine value planks to play off one another. Or how Apple's ecosystem of products and services integrate and work together.

Value Defined—What You Get for What You Pay

Value proposition development recognizes two basic ways to win: either lowering cost or differentiating through enhanced benefits. Value is defined by a simple formula, where it equals what you get for what you pay:

$$\text{Value} = \frac{\text{what you get}}{\text{what you pay}}$$

Value is increased either by adding benefits (i.e., value elements or planks) or reducing what customers pay through lower pricing. Often, companies do both—increasing what you get while decreasing what you pay. It typically makes sense to improve value by focusing on "what you get" unless the business is the absolute lowest cost provider.

Though it may seem like value elements are over-emphasized in this chapter (including the profile examples), these are the very things that create compelling propositions. The profile companies are excellent operators and understand customer delight is delivered through the details.

Also, consider that value is determined through the eyes of the customer—whether the benefits are rational or emotional, or tangible or perceived.

In both creating and tracking offering development, consider the role of a value proposition canvas.

CUSTOMER INSIGHT TIP

A value proposition canvas is a useful tool to both manage and quantify value planks, by tracking performance metrics. Here is a simplified illustration.

Online Retailer Value Proposition Canvas

Benefit Areas / Factors	Low	Brand Performance	High
Convenient shopping experience			
Variety and choice			
Speed and efficiency			
Free shipping and easy returns			
Consolidated media purchases			
Price			

Brand A = ·······●·······   Online Competitors = ·······▲·······

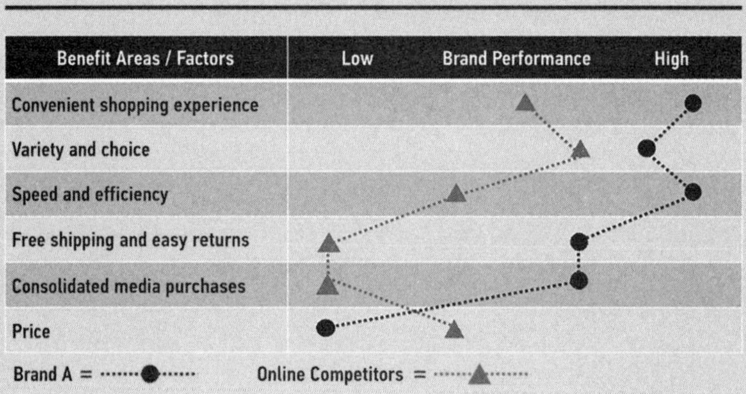

Figure 4.4

In this example, the benefit areas/factors in the left column are taken from the Amazon example from figure 4.2. Note Brand A's dominant performance across all factors, including benefit areas where competitor performance is nonexistent.

The value proposition canvas helps to visualize a company's or product's current strategic position and chart future strategies.

During internal strategy sessions, start with the "as is" canvas and then share a strawman "to be" version for reaction. This forces the team to think in terms of customer benefits (instead of existing product or services) and invites feedback. Quantitative research can then be used to map and manage client's brand performance across relevant metrics.

VALUE PROPOSITION EXAMPLES

Southwest Airlines

Southwest Airlines built its business keeping essential things simple and implementing them consistently. Southwest offers one plane type, one class of service, and no preassigned seats. It has a limited set of destinations, often at secondary, less congested airports. If you want to fly to Chicago, you'll find more flights to Midway than O'Hare. Jetting to New York? On Southwest, you'll likely land in LaGuardia, not JFK. At each airport, you *won't* be spending any time in Southwest Airlines' airport lounge. Southwest doesn't offer one.

Contrast this with major airlines like United, Delta, or American, which offer more amenities. Do some flyers value full-reclining leather seats, surround sound, four-star meals, and first-class treatment? Sure they do. Southwest just chooses not to target them.

Southwest targets a specific customer and aligns its people-first culture and business operations to deliver a winning experience (see figure 4.5).

Value Proposition Development

Southwest Case example

Consumer Need/Situation	Value Planks	Value Elements (Assets, Capabilities, Action)
Safely get from point A to B	Fun, Friendly Flying Experience	• Safe, clean planes • People-first culture • Intentional hiring
At a reasonable cost	Low Fares/Efficient Operations	• Secondary airports • One plane type • No meals
No hidden fees	"Tranfarency"	• Free checked bags • No change fees • Free live TV
Hassle-free travel, with no surprises	Simple Experience	• No first class • No assigned seats
Convenient schedule and purchase process	Convenience and Coverage	• Point-to-point (vs. hub & spoke) • Frequent departure times • Secondary (less congested) airports

Source: EquiBrand Consulting analysis

Figure 4.5

Let's dissect Southwest's five value planks. For many people, air travel is about getting from point A to B safely. These are table stakes needs, but also where Southwest excels through its "Fun, Friendly Flying Experience" plank. Southwest's industry-leading customer satisfaction and customer loyalty scores, delivered through its people, are clear differentiators.

Here's a personal example. All airlines are required to explain safety guidelines before departing. Most flight attendants drone on about the dos and don'ts before departing. One early morning, the Southwest flight attendant improvised this version: "Buckle your seat belts low and tight across your waist . . . (wait for it) . . . like J.Lo wears her pants."

That line struck more than a few people as funny that morning. Now when hearing, "Buckle your seat belts . . ." the Southwest version gets completed, if only in their heads, and gives a good feeling about the brand.

The added cost to Southwest for this real-life commercial and deepened customer connection? Other than keeping its employees happy and engaged, zero.

Southwest's next benefit plank, low fares/efficient operations, aligns internally with company operations and cost-saving measures. One example: Southwest uses only one plane type, the Boeing 737. Compare this with United, Delta, and American, who may operate ten or more types of aircraft.

Having one plane type results in lower maintenance and operational costs, which are passed on to consumers through lower fares.

The "Transfarency" plank delivers on the customer need for no surprises. Competitors charge to check baggage. On Southwest, you can check two bags for free. Competitors charge change fees. Southwest does not. Southwest also offers free live TV and all food is complimentary. This Transfarency plank represents a branded initiative for Southwest and is central to its positioning.

The simple experience plank provides a hassle-free experience. With no first-class section, Southwest streamlines food and beverage service. No assigned seats mean they fill quicker, with shorter plane time at the gate. Grabbing differentiation and efficiency where it can, Southwest resists the path of its competitors who instead squeeze more out of consumers.

The final value plank, convenience and coverage, is delivered through the company's point-to-point route structure, rather than the traditional hub-and-spoke model. Since secondary airports are less congested, Southwest minimizes ground time and improves performance. This allows for more direct nonstop routes and more frequent, conveniently timed flights.

While Southwest has low fares, it's often not the cheapest. Still, brand value is what you get for what you pay. By linking and aligning value planks—a motivated team, deep focus on the customer, and efficient operations—Southwest delivers a superior value proposition and financial performance that make it the envy of the industry.

Starbucks

Starbucks is a great example of how "commoditized" products can compete on value by stringing together a number of brand benefit planks.

At the most basic level, Starbucks markets three things: product, service, and atmosphere, crafted into a "third place" experience. It then combines these with a diversity, inclusion, and social impact plank to round out the offering.

Starbucks elevates the coffee-drinking experience well beyond a cup of joe for an estimated 60 million visitors per week who don't seem to mind spending $5 or so for a venti, skinny, vanilla latte or similar drink. Let's break down Starbucks' proposition, plank by plank (see figure 4.6).

Value Proposition Development

Starbucks Case example

Consumer Need/Situation	Value Planks	Value Elements (Assets, Capabilities, Action)
Great-tasting coffee to start the day	Best Coffee in the World	• Highest quality coffee, from top growers • Proprietary custom roasting process • Supply chain leadership
Service experience that feels like I'm valued	Uplifting Service Experience	• Customer intimacy (names, drink orders) • Mobile app digital engagement • Starbucks rewards program
Fits my community	Local Coffee House Ambiance	• Store designed to reflect neighborhood
A comfortable place between home and work	"Third Place" Experience	• Place away from home and the office • Free Wi-Fi, comfortable seats • Designed for work, study, socializing
A place I feel welcome and can trust	Diversity, Inclusion, & Social Impact	• Paid college tuition for partners • Community, ethical sourcing, environment • Racial bias training

Source: EquiBrand Consulting analysis

Figure 4.6

The first value plank ties to the core product—coffee—and sets a lofty goal: offer the best-tasting coffee in the world. Starbucks does this by controlling its supply chain—working directly with growers, overseeing its custom roasting process, and controlling retail distribution. Starbucks invests heavily here, given how vital this is to its business proposition.

Customer intimacy and personalization is the second plank. Starbucks seeks to deliver an uplifting experience with every customer, offered both personally and digitally.

Personally, baristas are trained to use customers' names, remember their drink orders, and have intentional conversations with them for a more intimate experience.

Digitally, through Starbucks' app and Wi-Fi service—patrons can order, pay ahead, and manage their rewards program.

It's not easy to provide a personal experience across roughly 30,000 stores, but Starbucks makes it a core value plank to direct both its people and company operations.

The third value plank centers on in-store ambiance, designed to reflect local culture and characteristics of each neighborhood. Starbucks avoids cookie-cutter store designs, knowing this adds to customer intimacy, builds loyalty, and solidifies the bond with its consumers.

The fourth plank recognizes that for many people, Starbucks is a comfortable "third place" (outside of home and work) to socialize and get stuff done.

Describing the strategy, Howard Schultz said, "Providing the world with a warm and welcoming third place may just be our most important role and responsibility, today and always."[45]

Ever the marketer, Schultz describes "third place" in terms of consumer benefits, but it's also a good business strategy. Offering a third place with free Internet, comfortable seating, and relevant menu options throughout the day also increases revenue at off-peak times.

The final plank speaks to Starbucks' diversity, inclusiveness, and social impact. These are employee-related values woven into every other aspect of the business. Howard Schultz said, "We built the Starbucks brand first with our people, not with consumers. Because we believed the best way to meet and exceed the expectations of our customers was to hire and train great people, we invested in employees."[46]

Nike

Nike's corporate proposition has changed over time to reflect the brand's shifting environment and business strategy.

In its early days, Nike emphasized three planks: product design, endorsements from star athletes, and brick and mortar distribution. In other words, create Air Jordans, have Michael promote them, and sell them at Foot Locker.

Relying on mall-based and emerging online retailers for distribution, though, left Nike one step removed from its consumers. Nike responded by expanding its focus on direct-to-consumer (DTC) activities, serving athletes one-on-one via digital technology and direct distribution.

Just like Amazon added Prime, Nike carved out Nike Membership (initially dubbed Nike Plus) to organize and combine its DTC efforts, including beefing up and integrating mobile apps and related tech-enabled offerings.

Creating a separate value proposition at a level below, but aligned with Nike's corporate proposition, allows Nike Membership to tap into corporate brand benefits while layering on other consumer-direct benefits (see figure 4.6).

Value Proposition Development

Nike Membership Case example

Consumer Need/Situation	Value Planks	Value Elements (Assets, Capabilities, Action)
Access to Nike products in one place	Nike Branded Shopping Experience	• Direct online access to Nike footwear and apparel products
Stay on top of what's new with Nike	Member-Exclusive Products	• Early access to new products • Exclusive access to member-only products • Favorite gear reserved in your size
Improve athletic performance	Expert Guidance & Advice	• Chat with real athletes to get recommendations on training and products
Connect me and my community	Connect to Sport, Anytime, Anywhere	• Access over 100 on-the-go workouts, weekly challenges, and personalized training plans
Expand and personalize my experience	One-of-a-Kind Experiences	• From courtside to race day, get priority access to events and sessions

Source: EquiBrand Consulting analysis

Figure 4.6

Nike Membership, which requires consumer email capture, integrates its fitness technology value elements all in one place, resulting in multiple benefits. Members reap the rewards, while Nike learns about consumer preferences and shopping habits to personalize future brand engagements.

Nike Membership is the enabling platform for Nike's consumer-direct offensive. It is central to Nike's DTC strategy as the company seeks to lead consumer fitness technology and grow its online sales.

BENEFITS OF A STRONG VALUE PROPOSITION

A strong value proposition offers numerous company and customer benefits. It:

Creates a multidimensional definition of brand value. The strongest offerings encompass a broad set of customer benefits in the form of value elements and planks. Many brands launch with a narrow range of benefits and then expand them over time. Consider that each plank provides an opportunity to innovate and enhance overall value. So, improve planks and expand their numbers. In general, the more benefits, the higher the perceived value.

Surrounds and deepens the relationship with end customers. Creating customer experiences that extend far beyond a product sale leads to enhanced brand value. Wherever possible, surround the consumer with touchpoints to broaden and deepen their experience. Like Amazon and Nike, move beyond the core offering and provide new features, subscriptions, quality cues, and digital integration.

Drives strategies and actions across the organization. Think of a value proposition as a statement of strategy—what the brand should stand for and deliver on. The one-page framework is a great tool to literally get the team on the same page strategically. Each functional department should ask how it can better align and integrate with other departments to unlock growth and improve customer value.

Provides strategic guideposts to focus innovation and assess opportunities. While brands are valuable assets that can and should be extended selectively (as described in the next chapter), there is a risk of stretching them too far. A strong value proposition helps identify opportunities and makes it easier to say no to initiatives that don't align.

What Makes a Strong Value Proposition?

Successful brands and businesses must be relevant to customers, be unique versus competitors, and be sustainable, as shown in figure 4.7.

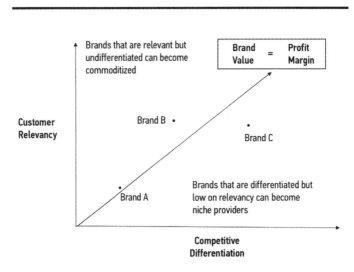

Figure 4.7

Ask the following questions when evaluating business propositions to ensure they clear three hurdles:

- **Relevance:** Do the value planks offer meaningful benefits to customers? Relevancy is the first-order requirement. If the value elements are not relevant, it doesn't matter how distinctive they are.

- **Distinctiveness:** Are the planks unique compared to other offerings in the marketplace? Not every value plank needs to be differentiated, but the sum of the whole must distinguish itself from competitor offerings.

- **Sustainability:** Can you credibly deliver the offering and make money, both today and in the future?

These same criteria are used to evaluate brand positionings, which is discussed in the next chapter.

HOW TO DESIGN AND ALIGN VALUE PROPOSITIONS

Creating a value proposition is more than organizing needs, benefits, and capabilities into a chart form. In some cases, it requires creating completely new business offerings—new companies, business models, products, and services—top to bottom. In others, it involves refining existing planks or establishing new ones. Here are some practical steps to design new offerings.

Step 1: Obtain Deep Customer Insight.

In Principle 1: Insight, we covered the need to define your purpose, look closer, think deeper, and establish the to-whom, for-what framework.

These inputs provide requisite consumer, marketplace, and technical insights for creating value propositions. What are the benefits customers seek, their trade-offs and friction points? What jobs do customers have that need to be done?

When creating value propositions, group similar needs, using the benefit hierarchy or ante, driver, reassurance framework explained in chapter 2.

Step 2: Define the Scope—At the Corporate, Business Unit, or Product Level.

Value propositions occur at multiple levels within an organization. Think Amazon versus Amazon Prime, Nike versus Nike Membership, or Disney versus Disney+.

In designing value propositions, if you can, start at the corporate level so these planks can then cascade down to division, category, and product levels, where they can be leveraged, modified, or supplemented with new ones to improve target-specific relevance.

This further promotes a clear identity and consistency across the organization.

Step 3: Unpack and Assess Individual Value Elements.

Unpacking and evaluating assets, capabilities, and actions helps uncover new opportunities.

Start by listing things like core competencies, brands, products, services, programs, and other elements of your business that add value. Does your organization have strong capabilities in technology, design, sourcing, logistics, or advanced manufacturing?

After unpacking individual value elements, consider assembling them in new ways to create new value. You may find your organization lacks specific capabilities, in which case plan to build or acquire them.

Also, consider the role new technologies—digital products, network models, and Internet-of-Things applications—might play in creating value.

Step 4: Ideate, Prototype, and Test Value Propositions.

Drawing on inputs from Steps 1–3, begin modifying existing or creating new value propositions, using focused ideation and iterative concept optimization. The process involves several sub-steps and is fully detailed in Principle 3: Innovation.

In the early stages, create and optimize concepts at the individual plank level. Then, combine them into the integrated whole. After initial feedback, refine ideas, moving from written concepts to drawings, mock websites, and physical prototypes. With greater confidence in the concept, allocate more resources to moving toward completion, iterating as you go.

The phrase "design thinking" is sometimes used to describe this process, which is further explored in chapter 6.

DESIGN THINKING IN UPSTREAM MARKETING

Design thinking is a concept used in strategy development that has gained broader acceptance within the business community. While the phrase is relatively new, the approach is not.

Walt Disney used design thinking to bring his ideas to life. This included brainstorming, storyboarding, and concept optimization—all standard methods in design thinking.

A case in point involved creating Snow White and the seven dwarfs—Scrappy, Dirty, Cranky, Sappy, Jumpy, Weepy, and Hungry. Did you catch that? These were some of the earlier possibilities the Disney development team considered before landing on Grumpy, Happy, Sleepy, Bashful, Sneezy, Doc, and Dopey.[47]

The core premise of design thinking is to solve problems creatively by beginning with the end in sight.

The process is iterative and can involve several rounds of ideation, prototyping, and testing. Customer feedback is obtained early and often, to reshape solutions and get closer to the final answer.

With its roots in product design and human factor engineering, design thinking has broad applications across marketing, product development, and

continued

other functions. Use it to build innovative products and systems and enhance the total customer experience.

While the profile companies may not explicitly use the phrase, design thinking is evident in the sleekness of an Apple device, the interior of a Starbucks store, and across Nike's product portfolio.

Their products have a clear design orientation, and this is carried over into how they conduct business.

Step 5: Align Your Organization to Deliver.

The final step in validating and launching new businesses includes filling operational gaps and aligning your organization to deliver.

Practically, this means working in tandem with cross-functional teams to understand, prioritize, and align internal initiatives with benefit planks.

Deliverables from this step include business strategy rationale (what worked and why), overarching strategic implications, prioritization of initiatives, and the plan to bring the value proposition to life.

MINI CASE EXAMPLE

It's conceivable to be so focused on end customers that you miss other factors in creating value propositions. We were hired by a mobile tech startup to help develop a consumer value proposition and brand strategy for a new mobile phone concept. The product concept was brilliant: a simple, five-button mobile phone so tweens and their parents could safely stay in touch. While families loved the idea, large phone carriers, which commanded over 90 percent of the market, had no interest in opening their infrastructure to the startup. The lesson: A well-designed value stack should consider and align all marketplace factors in operationalizing the offering.

VALUE PROPOSITION Q & A

Q: Is there a right number of value planks?

A: In general, the more value planks, the better. This is because customers typically prefer more, rather than fewer benefits. Still, adding benefits can get overly complicated and costly. While there is no target number of benefit planks, four to six is a good starting point.

This range offers customers enough value to derive benefits while providing the company with a reasonable set of planks to manage.

Also, it's better to develop fewer, more robust benefit planks than create too many that compete for your customers' attention. In other words, put more wood behind fewer arrows by combining individual value elements into broader plank ideas. Amazon and Southwest did this through Amazon Prime and Transfarency, respectively.

CUSTOMER INSIGHT TIP

Quantitative research can help determine the appeal of individual value planks and how they combine to represent the optimal set.

The basic idea is to measure the appeal of one value plank—first on its own, and then as part of the entire set—to understand the combined effect of the offering. In other words, how many people find a single value plank appealing? Then, after adding a new plank to the existing one, how many new customers are attracted to the offering?

continued

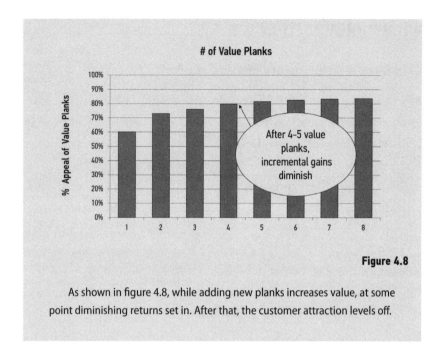

# of Value Planks

As shown in figure 4.8, while adding new planks increases value, at some point diminishing returns set in. After that, the customer attraction levels off.

Figure 4.8

The implication? Stop adding new benefits and invest elsewhere. Returns are unlikely to increase after a certain point.

Q: Is there a desired order to the planks?

A: Customers tend to consider and purchase complete value propositions rather than individual planks. Therefore, the plank order shouldn't matter. Internally, however, identifying the most critical planks first can help focus your organization.

Often one benefit—typically the category ante benefit—outsizes the rest in terms of customer appeal. Other planks then increase overall appeal, bring in new customers, or differentiate your organization from competitors.

Planks work best when they work as a team. One plank establishes the ante, additional planks differentiate from competitors, and another offers reassurance.

Consider a hypothetical example for Nike running shoes. Most of the value is in the product itself—what a runner laces up before heading out the door.

Let's say this contributes 70 percent of the utility—it's the main reason to purchase Nike. There is also value, though, with Nike Membership to inspire fitness and record workouts. Maybe this adds another 10 percent of the worth. Then there is the intangible value of the Nike brand, say another 5 percent tied to *Just Do It* and the emotional benefits associated with the brand. Layer on ancillary benefits and the Nike value proposition outperforms that of its competitors.

Of course, consumers don't actually calculate value this way, but it's a useful exercise for business leaders. The more you can do to elevate brand benefits, the better the overall value proposition for consumers.

Q: Do individual planks need to differentiate?

A: The short answer is no. It's the *combination* of value planks—the entire value stack—that must differentiate your organization from competitors.

Individual planks often operate at the ante or table stakes level: All banks need to offer easy access to your money, fast-food restaurants should be quick, convenience stores must be convenient. These benefits are required to get in the game, with limited opportunity for differentiation.

Value planks extending outside core category benefits provide the potential for distinctiveness. Figure 4.9 provides examples of value planks only tangentially related to the core that increased competitive differentiation.

Category	Value Plank	Capability/Action
Medical Devices	Patient education to help reduce anxiety with device implant	Standard-setting patient resources at every touchpoint (in office, online, at home, post-op)
Credit Cards	Extend membership privileges beyond standard services	Preferred seating at concerts and sporting events
Home Repair	More convenient scheduling to fit the way people live	Ability to track service calls online, with a guaranteed 2-hour service window
Packaged Food	Homemade taste with coffeehouse presentation	Online recipes with a few accessible mix-in ingredients instead of "just add water."

Figure 4.9

The key is uncovering customer needs, then using creative problem solving to define value planks and operational activities to support them. Find a need and fill it.

Q: Where's the cost plank?

A: While cost and pricing are important considerations, a separate cost plank is typically *not* part of a value proposition. Instead, price is the basis by which customers evaluate the *entire* offering. So, set cost aside, at least for a moment, and focus on value first.

You may find customers are willing to pay more than you initially thought for a combination of unique value elements. Use strategic pricing to deliver enhanced value through a good, better, best pricing model, for example.

Programs like subscription services, extended warranties and money-back guarantees can provide value perceptions that outweigh the cost of service. Ultimately, a cost-benefit analysis needs to be performed, though by elevating value perceptions, you can often obtain better pricing and higher margins.

Developing value propositions and making customers aware of them are related but separate concepts. It's possible to have a strong offering that is poorly communicated and nobody knows about.

In this case, a value proposition is like a light under a bushel—it cannot offer benefits if no one is aware it's there. In creating value propositions, it's equally important to develop a strong brand in support of the offering, as described next.

QUESTIONS TO CONSIDER

1. What value propositions are offered today at the corporate, division, and product level?

2. Is there alignment across customer needs, brand value planks, and company operations?

3. What opportunities exist to increase value by introducing new benefit planks or by surrounding the customer in more meaningful ways?

CHAPTER 5

BUILD AND EXTEND
THE BRAND

"You can't build a reputation on what you are going to do."
—Henry Ford, *founder, Ford Motor Company*

"If you are not a brand, you are a commodity."
—Philip Kotler, *author, consultant, and professor at Kellogg School
of Management, Northwestern University*

"Brands that do not see the future coming usually do not have one."
—Jean-Marie Dru, *global advertising veteran and author*

THINK OF NAPA VALLEY, AND you think of wine. Hollywood? It's synonymous with the motion picture industry. Silicon Valley is the center of digital technology and innovation. Think Central Indiana, and you think . . . Hmm.

For many people, Central Indiana—Indianapolis and its surrounding counties—has an image more associated with Indy Racing, manufacturing, cornfields, and cold winters than anything else. However, there's another side to Central Indiana—it has a strong, growing presence within the life sciences industry.

Corporately, Indianapolis is home to several global health-care organizations. These include pharmaceutical giant Eli Lilly, Roche Diagnostics, Anthem, Covance, Elanco, Corteva and other life sciences companies. Indiana-based companies Zimmer Biomet and Cook Group, located outside of Indianapolis, contribute rich assets to the region.

Academically, Central Indiana is home to Indiana University, Purdue University, and other higher educational institutions. IU School of Medicine, firmly based in Indianapolis, is the largest and a top-ranked medical school in the United States each year. Just over an hour's drive away, in West Lafayette, there's Purdue College of Pharmacy and the College of Engineering, which offer programs in biological and biomedical engineering.

As a place to live and work, Indianapolis consistently receives top-tier status in published rankings. It has professional sports teams, unique neighborhoods, affordable living, and a family-focused community.

Central Indiana, for some though, has an identity problem. On the one hand, it possesses tremendous assets on which to build. On the other, its brand image is inconsistent with this reality.

Due in part to its image perception, local life science businesses had a tough time attracting and retaining talent to drive growth. Recent graduates from local colleges were heading to the East and West coasts. These new, highly educated graduates perceived greater opportunities elsewhere, unaware that much of what they sought was already in their community.

Community leaders, concerned about the effects of this "brain drain" on the economy, decided to establish an initiative to address it. Central Indianapolis Life Sciences Initiative (CILSI) was formed, made up of top leaders from local corporations, academic institutions, and local government.

Based on prior EquiBrand work with several local companies, we were called in to help strategically market the region.

Our initial assessment confirmed that while the area had tremendous assets, it lacked an organizing mechanism to integrate them.

It was analogous to having the frame, seat, handlebars, chain, and tires—but no bicycle.

Constructing an initial benefit hierarchy helped identify potential features and attributes on which to build a compelling brand story. Figure 5.1 offers a partial view of that hierarchy.

Central Indiana Life Sciences Initiative

Benefits: What does that do for me?	Benefit A		Benefit B		Benefit C	
	Central Indiana Life Sciences Functional Attributes					
Functional Attributes: What are they?	Corporate Assets	Academic Assets	Access to Capital	Innovation Infrastructure	"Indy Appeal"	Educated Workforce

Figure 5.1

It became clear that a new brand could serve as a "mental file folder" for the initiative, allowing people to attach associations in a way they historically had not. But what was the overall concept? Who should be targeted? For what needs? What was the value proposition and brand concept to tie it together?

After team analysis, we selected the entrepreneurial community as the bull's-eye target. This decision was a bit controversial, as entrepreneurs were not well funded at the time. Building the brand from this lens, though, would promote clarity and consistency. A clear target helped rally the team and served as a unifying platform for building the brand.

From there, we used internal workstreams, including strategy sessions and focused ideation, to build out a value proposition and brand strategy concepts. A dozen or so verbal concepts were developed and iterated throughout the project.

We tested ideas with everyone from civic, academic, and industry leaders to college students, recent grads, and startup executives using the CORE methodology described earlier.

We attended scientific sessions at a trade show, conducted qualitative research from behind a one-way mirror, and held informal pizza party discussions at local universities. Here is the winning concept statement:

BIOCROSSROADS—ACCELERATING THE FORMATION AND GROWTH OF LIFE SCIENCES BUSINESSES AT THE CROSSROADS OF AMERICA

America's heartland is fast becoming a major source of breakthrough research and discovery into medical devices, diagnostics, pharmaceuticals, and agrosciences. Indiana is a place where medical, engineering, and pharmaceutical research institutions and businesses come together, along with the advanced manufacturing and distribution capabilities those disciplines require.

Now Indiana is using the synergy of that business, government, and academic convergence to accelerate the development and growth of new life sciences businesses.

BioCrossroads was created to be a catalyst for building the region's entrepreneurial capacity. Helping entrepreneurs plug into the area's network of specialized resources and experienced professional support is an initiative priority. Whether you need business accelerator resources—like financial or legal services, lab space, or business planning—or want access to the academic community's world-class pool of life sciences or engineering talent, BioCrossroads provides an open door and helps make the network accessible.

Here, at the crossroads of America, life sciences businesses have the opportunity—and the encouragement—to flourish.

Coming out of the research, we led additional strategy sessions with the client team to build the brand. Activities included finalizing the name as well as downstream-related aspects—building the brand identity, setting graphic standards (logo use, type, color, etc.), creating a website, collateral materials, and more.

An action plan for launching the brand was developed, identifying and aligning opportunities for promoting the brand through public relations, advertising, and events.

BioCrossroads was launched later that year and continues to be successful today. Indiana is recognized as one of the top states in the nation for the life sciences industry, while before this effort, it was in the bottom quartile. Over $250 million was secured in new capital formation, with numerous industry, government, and university partnerships formed. Business growth is up, based on tech transfers, startups, and organic growth.

In 2020, life sciences contributed over $75 billion in economic value to Indiana, and the state is the second largest exporter of life sciences products in the US. Today there are over 2,100 life sciences businesses in Indiana, geographically clustered around Indianapolis and scattered across the state. Two new assets BioCrossroads helped create include the Indiana Biosciences Research Institute and 16 Tech innovation district. All told, the region has one of the largest arrays of life science companies and jobs in the nation, with BioCrossroads serving as the catalyst for growth and innovation.

BioCrossroads is a case study in how to create a brand from scratch: obtain customer insight, iterate value proposition concepts, and establish a strong positioning as the platform for downstream implementation.

BRAND BUILDING AT PROFILE COMPANIES

Take a minute and think about your favorite Starbucks TV commercial, radio jingle, or billboard. Then, consider the cleverness of the Amazon television advertising campaign or magazine ad. Or recall the latest Google promotion or frequent clickers program.

It's not easy, is it? Mainly because these companies have built their brands upstream and do comparatively little downstream marketing: They eschew taglines, jingles, and celebrity endorsers.

Howard Schultz views the Starbucks brand this way: "We look at the brand not as a piece of advertising, but everything we do communicates who Starbucks is. The place, the physical environment really has become an extension of the brand and it's very important to the success of the company." Schultz continues, "Starbucks is not an advertiser; people think we are a great marketing company, but in fact we spend very little money on marketing and more money on training our people than advertising."

Schultz warns about outsourcing brand development or relegating it too low within the organization: "Authentic brands don't emerge from marketing cubicles or advertising agencies. They emanate from everything the company does."[48]

Jeff Bezos, of Amazon, defines brand this way: "Your brand is what people say about you when you're not in the room."[49] This sentiment is consistent with the idea of looking at your business through the eyes of your customers. In other words, a brand is how others perceive you based on *their* experiences—not on what *you* say about it or what you'd like it to be.

When Southwest undertook a massive rebranding effort across the company, its leadership was quick to point out what *didn't* change. "Southwest unveils its new look, same heart," was the title of the press release. CEO Gary Kelly said, "The Heart emblazoned on our aircraft, and within our new look, symbolizes our commitment that we'll remain true to our core values as we set our sights on the future."[50] Southwest's core remains, updated with a new brand look and feel.

The strongest, most enduring brands result from the disciplined alignment of brand strategies and plans with customer requirements. Like value propositions, branding can occur at multiple levels—corporate, division, product, and so forth. In this way, a company like Walt Disney may have thousands of branded assets, each representing individual value propositions.

WHAT IS A BRAND?

There are numerous ways to define a brand. At the corporate level, consider the brand as the face you put on your business strategy. This idea flows from the concept that the corporate vision is the eyes, the mission is the heart, and the brand is an external expression of these to customers, employees, and investors. It's how you present your business to others. A brand is a relationship a company has with its customers.

A more academic definition is that a brand is comprised of associations that individuals attribute to a product or service or company.

As shown in figure 5.2, a brand is more than a product, with brand equity providing the added value. Some consider a brand as everything that's left over when you set the product aside. Remove the logo from a Starbucks cup, and how different really, is the product inside of it?

Products			Brands		
			Nike	Apple	Starbucks
• Functional benefits			• Functional and emotional benefits		
• Made in a factory			• Exists in the minds and hearts of customers		
• Can be objectively measured and evaluated			• Difficult to objectively evaluate		

Figure 5.2

Here's another way to think about it. Figure 5.3 has images of two products. The one on the top is a fiddle, and the one on the bottom is a violin.

First, imagine the fiddle, the fiddler playing it, and the crowd who might be listening. What images come to mind? Close your eyes if it's helpful. Now, imagine the same for the violin, violinist, and the people in the audience. What do you see?

Figure 5.3

If you're like most people, the images in your mind's eye for the fiddle and the violin differ. The fiddle conjures imagery of folk and country music, and maybe cowboy hats, flannel shirts, and denim.

The violin makes you think of classical music, formal wear, and a night on the town. Now, consider that the fiddle and the violin are the exact same bowed instrument. It's the same product, but with different associations.

This example speaks to the role brand imagery plays in aligning to the target customer, shaping perceptions, creating differentiation, and extracting value.

Nike, Apple, Starbucks, and the other profile companies create compelling brand identities to resonate with customers and differentiate from competitors, with the end goal of driving profitable growth.

WHY INVEST IN BRAND BUILDING?

A strong brand generates superior profits by maximizing volume and price potential in a product or category. Consider the following example, which tested two soft drink products, first unbranded, then branded. In this case, as shown in figure 5.4, Cola B was able to overcome a gap in product preference, versus Cola A, due to its stronger brand.

Why Invest in Brand Building?

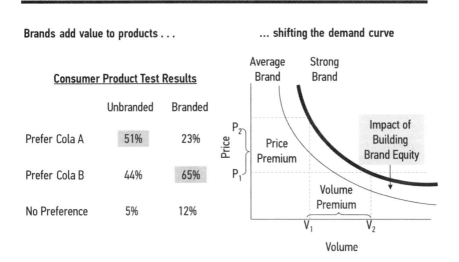

Figure 5.4

For customers, brands provide choice, simplify decisions, provide quality assurance, and facilitate risk avoidance. There are numerous benefits to brands, as they allow an organization to:

- Differentiate from the competition to provide for premium pricing, beyond commoditization

- Enhance credibility for new product introductions and keep customers in the brand family

- Increase return on marketing dollars by creating an umbrella brand over other offerings

- Send positive messages to shareholders and stakeholders, and attract and retain outstanding employees

Internally, brands serve as a guiding light to make strategic recommendations for where to allocate resources.

In defining a brand, it's sometimes useful to consider what a brand *is not*. A brand *is not* a name, logo, or tagline, although these are tangible things that might represent the brand.

MINI CASE EXAMPLE

It's conceivable a brand can have negative equity that does more harm than good. We were hired by an automotive client who made wonderful cars, though they had a poor brand image due to decades old, lingering quality concerns.

To assess brand impact for a new product launch, consumers were asked to test drive a new vehicle "unbranded," with the logo-badge on the front of the car and other details covered up. Potential customers were then asked how much they'd expect to pay for the vehicle, which averaged roughly $25,000.

Consumers in a control group then drove the exact same vehicle, only this time with the client's brand and identifying features visible. With these consumers, the anticipated purchase price dropped to $22,250, or a reduction of 10 percent. In this case, the brand image negatively affected brand value, resulting in need for proactive brand management.

BRAND MIGRATION

The BioCrossroads case involved *creating* a brand from scratch. In most cases, brands already exist in the minds of customers, so it's more about *migrating* a brand by strengthening and extending it over time. Brands are dynamic and should be continually nurtured. In evolving existing brands, consider three points in time, as shown in figure 5.5.

Brand Migration Management

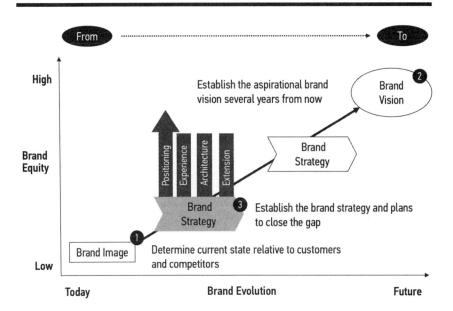

Figure 5.5

Point 1 is the current brand image, determined through a brand audit. How do customers view the brand today—its strengths and weaknesses—compared to competitors?

Point 2 is the desired future state. What does the brand aspire to be several years from now? Are there new products or services on the horizon that might affect brand trajectory? Does the brand need to take on new associations to better fit target needs?

Point 3 represents the gap between the current state (1) and the ideal future state (2). The role of brand strategy and development, then, is closing the gap. It does this using four components, as discussed next.

FOUR KEYS TO BRAND MANAGEMENT

1. **Brand positioning** is the conceptual place you want to own in the target customer's mind—the benefits you want them to think of when they consider your brand.

2. **Brand-customer experience** represents the totality of how customers interact with your business and brand—the touch-points they encounter within their journey.

3. **Brand architecture** is the logical, strategic, and relational structure of all products and brands in the portfolio.

4. **Brand extension** results from stretching established brand names into new products or new product categories.

CUSTOMER INSIGHT TIP

In crafting brand strategy components, including alternative positioning concepts, use the CORE method described in chapter 2 to create, test, and learn among alternatives. Clear brand communication is often the best, easiest, and least expensive way to increase customer engagement and grow your business.

Brand Positioning

At the core of the most valuable brands is a clear, succinct expression of the brand's positioning, supported by a portfolio of messages and touchpoints that align with that positioning. The brand positioning is an internal statement used to inform and reflect internal decision-making and external associations across the following: (see figure 5.6).

Figure 5.6

There are at least four ways to position a brand. The most common is to position on a category or product benefit. A benefit-based positioning is effective if the brand is the category leader or if viable white space areas exist where no other brand occupies a similar perceptual position. Here are profile company examples:

- **Position and own the category benefit.** Disney recognizes that consumers have many choices for travel and entertainment—the competitive frame extends well beyond amusement parks. Therefore, Disney delivers an experience unlike any other, positioning the park brand as "The Happiest Place on Earth."

- **Position how the company does business.** Southwest strings together several business practices into its "Transfarency" positioning. This positioning emphasizes value and leverages how the company does business into a meaningful benefit. Southwest then delivers on the positioning by aligning a host of operationally-driven customer benefits.

- **Position the product and the consumer.** Nike's "Just Do It" doesn't mention athletic shoes or even athletic performance. Instead,

Nike taps into the personal aspiration of its target consumer. Nike operates higher on the benefit hierarchy, offering more emotional and self-expressive benefits.

- **Position against the competition.** Apple's "Think Different" indirectly references competitors by citing how the company does things distinctively. Apple considered, but rejected, "Think Differently," favoring "different" instead. This decision resulted in more than a few online discussions regarding whether the phrase is grammatically correct. Which, at some level, reinforces the point.

In considering alternative positioning strategies, note a few points: First, it's not necessary to position on a single benefit, but do position on a single idea (Miller Lite's classic "Great Taste, Less Filling" positioning, while listing two benefits, was cleverly crafted into a single idea).

Also, don't confuse brand positioning with a brand tagline, despite the sample taglines being used here to express the positioning. A tagline is an outgrowth of the positioning, used to convey it in consumer communication.

Finally, while a brand's positioning should be reasonably enduring, it can (and often should) evolve to reflect market changes, including new competitors, new technological advances, and additional benefits sought.

CREATING A BRAND POSITIONING

A brand positioning should align with the value proposition and bring focus and clarity to brand-building tactics. We use the following template in developing a positioning, breaking it down into its essential components:

To (target audience), Brand X is the only (category or frame of reference) that gives/offers you (points of differentiation/benefits delivered) because (reasons to believe).

Positioning development involves the art of sacrifice. Choices must be made across four elements as described here:

Brand Positioning Strategic Choices

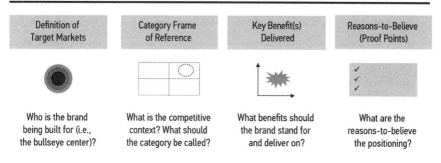

Definition of Target Markets	Category Frame of Reference	Key Benefit(s) Delivered	Reasons-to-Believe (Proof Points)
Who is the brand being built for (i.e., the bullseye center)?	What is the competitive context? What should the category be called?	What benefits should the brand stand for and deliver on?	What are the reasons-to-believe the positioning?

Figure 5.7

An effective brand positioning must meet the same objectives used to evaluate value propositions: relevancy, differentiation, and sustainability. Relevant but undifferentiated brands risk commoditization. Brands that are differentiated but irrelevant risk becoming niche providers. A winning proposition is one that is relevant, distinctive, and credible.

VERBAL AND VISUAL BRANDING IN IDENTITY DEVELOPMENT

In building a powerful brand, it's useful to make the distinction between verbal and visual branding. While both need to work together, it can help to think about them first alone and then in combination. Ad agencies and content

continued

creators often approach branding this way: A copywriter works out the verbal brand while the art director handles the visual aspects.

Verbal branding has to do with your brand's positioning, associations, story, content messaging, tagline, and the keywords you'll use to get found online. It should balance internal perspectives—the aspirations of your company—and external perspectives—the needs of your customers.

Visual branding encompasses the look and feel of the brand. Do you want to project the image of a small, neighborhood business or a much larger, professional firm? A craft-like or corporate experience?

The logo, imagery, website, marketing materials, and other visual aspects impact perceptions. Have a clear point of view and a consistent design aesthetic so everything works together.

Separating verbal and visual branding helps ensure focus on both components. Ultimately, the two parts come together in final creative materials—packaging, advertising, or website—with one complementing the other. The whole is greater than the sum of the parts.

The explosion in marketing content and brand storytelling has only heightened the need to establish a clear positioning.

In an era when marketers jockey to elevate Google search engine rankings and customers seek genuine brand connections, it's easy to diminish brand positioning as an archaic solution to yesterday's problem.

In our experience, though, brand positioning is foundational to business success and even more important today. Messaging and tactics will change over time, but brands should endure. So, be clear about the brand positioning. This will make brand strategy decisions, from touchpoint alignment and marketing communications to content marketing and brand storytelling, that much easier.

Once the positioning and related verbal and visual elements are established, create the brand development brief (also called a creative brief). This one- to two-page document should articulate the positioning, benefits sought, and brand story. Think of it as the blueprint for directing downstream efforts across creative and other implementation partners.

Brand positioning tends to focus on *what* is developed and delivered to customers. Top marketers recognize that *how* something is communicated—and *how* it's delivered operationally—can be equally important. This is the role of the brand-customer experience, as described next.

Brand-Customer Experience

One of EquiBrand's first clients was a manufacturer of pacemakers, defibrillators, stents, and other medical devices used by cardiologists and cardiac surgeons.

The company formed when a global pharmaceutical giant acquired separate device companies and merged them under a new business entity. We were called in by the newly appointed head of global marketing to "launch a new corporate brand" to unify the business and increase corporate value.

A few months prior to our involvement, the client had hired a large New York–based ad agency that specialized in consumer marketing. The agency researched patients with heart disease to understand their situation.

The insight? The company's products provided patients with both rational and emotional benefits, including a new outlook on life. The agency's creative team used the insight to create a two-minute video—the kind that tugs at your heart—to introduce the brand with the tagline "The Gift of Life."

Along with the new creative materials, the agency proposed an aggressive, multimillion-dollar, direct-to-consumer (DTC) campaign, approaching $10 million in TV and other mass advertising.

The new marketing head, unsure about the agency's proposal, asked our opinion on the DTC approach. We had some questions:

How are the products purchased? What are the purchasing criteria? We also mapped the customer journey and brand touchpoints, from diagnosis to post-procedure, and then prepared our findings.

Our recommendation: "Save the $9,900,000. Invest $100,000 in a consumer-directed brochure and redirect spending to professional marketing." The company had no business creating a direct-to-consumer brand as the consumer had no bearing on the purchase decision. Physicians and hospital buying committees bought the products. Patients were unaware of the brand and had no impact on brand choice.

So, while the campaign would have generated good feelings about the brand among patients, it would have done nothing to drive sales. Instead, we recommended a touchpoints strategy targeting physicians when and where they were receptive to brand messaging—at medical conferences and through trade journals, plus online and traditional in-office sales channels.

We also developed a consumer-directed program to help physicians inform their patients about healthy living habits. In the end, the brand image improved with its physician targets, and the education program positively impacted patients' lives.

CREATING THE BRAND-CUSTOMER EXPERIENCE

Brand-customer experience is how customers interact with your business through touchpoints along the decision journey. Think about the customer experience with Apple, Southwest, Starbucks, or The Walt Disney Company. Every interaction—advertising, website, in-store browsing, product packaging, and customer service—represents a brand touchpoint that can either enhance or detract from the experience.

Like other aspects of upstream marketing, establishing the ideal brand-customer experience requires looking at the business through the eyes of the customer. A customer journey map is a great tool for understanding and improving the experience. Figure 5.8 offers an example of a simplified journey map.

Customer Journey Mapping

		Pre-Purchase		Purchase		Post-Purchase	
		Awareness	Interest	Purchase	Delivery	Retention	Advocacy
Customer Need/ Situation • Thinking • Doing • Feeling							
Brand Touchpoints	Advertising						
	Website						
	Phone						
	In Person						
	Email						
	Other						
Ideas for Improvement							

Elements of the Customer Journey

Figure 5.8

The process for creating the optimal brand-customer experience involves several steps.

Step 1: Understand the "as is" journey.

Start by documenting the current journey by which customers become aware of, purchase, and experience your brand.

Consider the entire experience, from pre-purchase to purchase to post-purchase (or before, during, and after in colloquial terms). A variety of consumer behavior models exist, moving from awareness, familiarity, and preference to purchase and afterward. Actual customer journeys vary by category and are typically nonlinear, so tailor them to the situation.

Use customer research and internal workshops to review, create, and validate journey maps. Ask: What is the complete end-to-end journey by which customers interact with the brand today? What are the pain and gain points? What are customers thinking, doing, and feeling at each stage in the journey?

CUSTOMER INSIGHT TIP

Conversion metrics are a great way to quantitatively assess improvement opportunities along the purchase funnel. For example, track how customers are feeling and reacting to your brand at key points in their journey. How many customers are aware of your brand? What percentage of aware customers go on to purchase and repurchase? How many of these are retained? These metrics help isolate journey leverage points to improve upon.

Step 2: Create the ideal "to be" experience.

Next, create a vision of the ideal, including changes to the current system. Use sticky notes, flip charts, a dry-erase board, or software to show the current flow and signal improvements through a redesigned process. At each touchpoint—advertising, website, in-store, customer service—brainstorm the winning experience. What's ideal? What are friction points? Can we remove them? Draw on customer and technical insight to close the gaps.

Consider, for example, the way Amazon has elevated customer expectations in general. Examine how technology has transformed the way people learn about, purchase, and interact with Apple's products. Or how the Southwest app streamlines everything from booking flights, to checking in, monitoring flight status, and tracking customer rewards.

In creating the ideal customer experience, push beyond common convenience expectations of fast and easy. Starbucks delivers a relatively fast cup of coffee. What loyal customers covet are "quality cues," including sensory and experiential benefits. Starbucks masterfully plans and engages all five senses in a single visit: the aroma when you enter the store (smell), the warm, inviting ambiance (sight), baristas greeting you by name (sound), a warm cup in your hand (touch), and the product payoff (taste).

Some consumers favor a digital experience, others a more personal one. Many want both. The bar continues to rise, so examine new media and technologies for additional approaches.

Step 3: Align brand touchpoints to improve the experience.
Creating the ideal experience involves planning and integrating brand touchpoints across the journey. Implementation may require significant changes across marketing channels (e.g., website, mobile, face-to-face), media, messaging, and other efforts to sync with customer requirements.

Consider the Pareto principle in change management: How can you achieve an 80 percent improvement in customer experience through a 20 percent investment?

Brand Architecture

Step back for a moment and look at a company's brand portfolio through the eyes of the customer. Is it clear how various brands and products fit together? Or is there an opportunity to improve the brand presentation to improve clarity, synergy, and leverage?

Brand architecture is the third brand strategy component and recognizes that customers relate to brands at different levels, from the corporate brand to product brands, product descriptors, and so on.

Apple is an excellent example of a winning brand architecture, using a mix of brands and sub-brands, as summarized in figure 5.9.

Apple

| iMac | iPhone | iPad | Apple TV | Apple WATCH | Apple MUSIC |

MacBook
MacBook Pro
MacBook Air

Figure 5.9

Apple delivers on the three goals of effective brand architecture—clarity, synergy, and leverage.

- **Clarity:** Brand architecture must promote clarity—is it clear how everything fits together? Apple serves as the master brand, at the top, and encompasses product brands beneath it. Apple carries emotional benefits, while product brands—iMac, iPhone, iPad, and so on—convey more rational benefits and target-specific relevance. Finally, individual products are aligned underneath: iPad, iPad Pro, iPad Air, and iPad Mini.

- **Synergy:** Brand architecture allows the organization to deliver a larger promise than any single brand can achieve alone. Combining brands and sub-brands results in greater corporate value for all. Apple adds value to the iPhone, and iPhone adds value to Apple.

- **Leverage:** A well-managed architecture allows for extending brands both horizontally and vertically to capture new customer segments and markets. With the iPhone, Apple brought new users into the Mac franchise, and vice versa. iPod paved the way for the iPhone. The iPhone SE targeted a younger, value-conscious consumer.

Figure 5.10 shows Amazon's architecture. Notice how it also incorporates a hybrid approach, focusing on Amazon but using endorsed and stand-alone brands where their strength permits this.

Amazon

Sub-brands	Endorsed brands	Stand-alone brands	Business-to-Business
Amazon.com	Audible	Zappos.com	Amazon Web Services
Prime Video	Kindle Direct Publishing	Whole Foods	
Amazon Kindle		Ring	
Amazon Echo	Pill Pack by Amazon Pharmacy		

Figure 5.10

PRODUCT PORTFOLIO VS BRAND ARCHITECTURE

Product portfolio and brand architecture management are separate, though related concepts.

Product portfolio management addresses how a company can use its products and brands to achieve growth, drawing on the demand framework. The perspective is inside-out, considering company goals and objectives. An automotive example: Should we develop an electric vehicle?

Brand architecture management addresses how a company can best structure and communicate its portfolio of brands. The starting point is outside-in, through the eyes of the customer. In launching the new vehicle, should we create a new sub-brand (like Toyota did with Prius) or attach it to an existing one (like Honda Accord Hybrid)?

FOUR PRIMARY BRAND ARCHITECTURE MODELS

In establishing a brand architecture, there are four basic models on a spectrum, ranging from a branded house to a house of brands. Figure 5.11 shows an overview, using automotive brands.

Branded House	Sub-brand	Endorsed Brands	House of Brands
BMW **3 Series** **7 Series** **BMW X1**	**Honda** Civic C-RV Accord	**BMW | MINI**	**Chevrolet GMC** **Cadillac Buick**
Uses a single master brand and descriptors • Leverages established brand equity with minimal investment behind new offerings • Strong potential for economies of scale Typically, the default, go-to strategy	Sub-brands add to or modify associations of the master brand • They may have a different value proposition, positioning, and brand identity • A sub-brand can stretch the master brand to new arenas	Endorser brands provide credibility to the endorsed brand • An endorsed brand is linked with the endorser, though has freedom to develop associations and a brand identity different from that of the endorser	Contains a set of stand-alone brands, each focusing on a market segment • Can position clearly on desired benefits and dominate niche segments • Useful for avoiding incompatible associations
• BMW is the master brand with models denoted as BMW 3, BMW 7, BMW X1, BMW M, etc.	• Honda Accord and Toyota Camry are examples	• Mini is associated with BMW though has perceptual distance	• General Motor brands include Chevrolet, Buick, GMC, Cadillac

Figure 5.11

Defining the optimal structure is not an either/or decision. Most companies use a "hybrid" approach, mixing and matching the four models to suit their needs. This is often preferred as it tailors the solution to the industry, company, and customer situation.

A TREND TOWARD A BRANDED HOUSE APPROACH

A best practice in brand architecture management is to invest in the fewest number of brands needed to meet business goals. This recognizes the expense and complexity of creating and managing brands.

For this reason, there has been a shift toward building a powerful master brand and then using generic descriptors to name offerings.

In this case, the master brand is elevated and extended over other brands to achieve economic leverage. This approach maximizes resources behind one brand (puts more wood behind one arrow) and minimizes brand confusion and unnecessary proliferation.

With a branded house, it's typically best to *describe* or *name* rather than *brand* individual offerings. Here's the distinction:

- *Names* are simple descriptors that serve to identify the tangible value the consumer receives.

- *Brands* require investment and management and represent a value greater than the functionality of the offering alone.

In this default strategy, the master brand is used in concert with generic, non-branded product descriptors to promote clarity.

Google uses this naming approach with Google Maps, Google Drive, Google Earth, and Google Pay. Granted, YouTube has its own brand name, retained from its acquisition. But a case could have been made for calling it Google Videos.

ESTABLISHING CLEAR BRAND ROLES

While a branded house is often preferred, there are cases when a *portfolio of brands* makes sense. In these instances, distinct brands may play specialized roles, much like the positions on a sports team.

Amazon invests in numerous strategic brands—Amazon.com, Prime, Echo, and Kindle. These brands have clear targets and value propositions and represent meaningful sales and profits in the future.

Other company brands, Amazon Basics, Amazon Essentials, and Goodthreads in apparel—play targeted roles at a lower level, tied to value tiers. Amazon 1-Click serves as a branded feature that signifies shopping efficiency. All told, Amazon has hundreds of different trademarks, each with its own target consumer and value proposition.

When managing multiple brands, consider the relative investment required. Launching a strategic brand (Amazon Prime) can be a multimillion-dollar proposition. Creating a branded differentiator (1-Click) can be considerably less costly.

Of course, nobody sets out to create a confusing brand architecture. Complexity, though, can set in when business managers seek to create excitement behind a new product offering or when one company acquires another. Brands not adequately managed and invested in risk becoming "empty vessels" with no real meaning in the marketplace. In these cases, it's necessary to clean up the architecture to present a clear portfolio.

BRAND ARCHITECTURE MANAGEMENT STEPS

There is no magic formula or black-box approach to brand architecture management. Consider best practices, pros and cons analysis, and business judgment in creating and deciding among alternatives. Here are the steps:

Step 1: Obtain customer framework and business strategy inputs.
Creating the optimal brand portfolio architecture involves determining the number of brands required and their scope. How expansive should the brand be across customer segments, channels, and price points?

As discussed in chapter 3, most categories have clustered preferences, informed by the customer demand framework. Product portfolio management is internally focused. Brand architecture is customer-facing—how they might view your brands in-store or on a website. The two parts ultimately need to align.

Step 2: Confirm the "as is" brand architecture.

Inventory all brands across all touchpoints—the website, marketing material, advertising, uniforms, and signage. Create a "war room" to visually display what customers see and experience. Are there too many brands or not enough? Are there empty-vessel brands that should migrate to product descriptors?

Step 3: Obtain market and internal input to inform decisions.

Research the following factors (ideally, quantitatively) to inform decision making:

- Brand strength: What are current brand associations, and how strong are existing brand equities?

- Customer bandwidth: How many brands can customers understand?

- Strategic decisions: Do particular circumstances (e.g., partnerships) dictate tighter or looser brand linkages?

- Financial resources: How many brands can the organization afford to support?

Step 4: Develop alternative "to be" approaches.

When considering alternative brand hierarchies, focus on the desired perceptual distance between offerings. Use sticky notes to visualize alternatives. Don't worry whether the approach favors a house of brands versus branded house or employs a "sub-brand," "endorsed brand," or "driver brand." These terms can get in the way of a sound structure. Focus first on the desired architecture, and then apply the terms at the very end.

Step 5: Confirm brand architecture principles, hierarchy, and naming tree.

Once the brand architecture is confirmed, document and codify decisions as they are made. This will ensure future choices are on strategy and the overall objective of brand clarity, synergy, and leverage is achieved.

In the end, consider how customers experience the brand portfolio. In their eyes, is it clear how the brands fit together? Often, companies have sophisticated, matrixed organizations internally, which creep into brand presentation. Avoid this. Like ducks on a pond, strive to promote clarity and elegance externally, even though you might be paddling like crazy underneath to move forward.

Brand Extension

Brand extension—also called brand stretch—is the final component of brand strategy and a departure point in moving from the identity principle to the innovation principle. Brand extension recognizes that brands are valuable assets that can and should selectively extend to new business areas.

Rather than build a brand from scratch, stretch existing ones to new categories. This provides economic leverage, increasing the chance of new business success while also reducing cost. Other benefits of stretching brands include immediate awareness, accelerated trial, distribution leverage, and spending efficiencies.

Countless examples exist where brands have effectively extended into new categories. When done right, it's a win-win. Successful extensions build upon the equities of the parent brand and the entire portfolio benefits.

Starbucks' cold Frappuccino blended beverage is a great extension. Frappuccino strongly associates with coffee but brings in non-coffee drinkers.

This extension changed the trajectory of the company, filling stores in afternoons and during warm weather when coffee business is slow.

More recently, the company created Starbuck Refreshers, attracting tea drinkers during similar time periods.

Howard Schultz said, "Our history is based on extending the brand to categories within the guardrails of Starbucks and not abuse the trust people have by going off and doing things not consistent with the heritage of coffee."[51]

BRAND EXTENSION EXAMPLES	
Original brand	**Extended to**
Amazon	Amazon Prime, Kindle, Echo, Basics (private label)
Apple computers	Apple phones, tablets, watches, peripheral products, and content development and streaming
Disney animation	Disney merchandising, music, publishing, filmed entertainment, theme parks, vacation, resorts and property management, broadcasting, live entertainment, and digital properties
Nike running shoes	Nike footwear, apparel, and equipment across numerous categories
Starbucks coffee	Starbucks hot chocolate, mugs, tumblers, and presses, Frappuccino, and other food and beverage products

BRAND EXTENSION APPROACHES

Brands can be highly elastic—the key is not to violate the "essence" of the brand. There are two basic ways to extend brands. The first involves logical extension, where consumers naturally follow the brand to related categories. If you wear Nike running shoes and need tennis shoes, chances are you'll at least consider Nike. It's a logical extension from one category to the next.

The second approach uses equity bridges that marketers create for consumers to cross. Nike used this strategy to enter golf equipment, with Tiger Woods serving as an equity bridge for its clubs, balls, and related equipment (categories the company would later exit).

The reasoning: if it's good enough for Tiger, it's good enough for me. Without Tiger's endorsement, it would have been hard for Nike to enter those categories. Figure 5.12 gives a recap of the two broad approaches.

Two Basic Approaches to Brand Extension

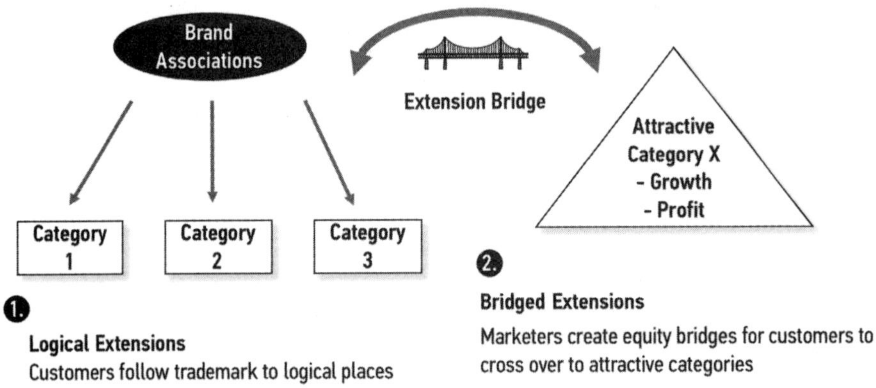

Figure 5.12

While both approaches can be successful, the second requires more focus but offers a higher potential payoff. Companies extending into further-out categories are rewarded with greater business growth. Brand elasticity begets elasticity. The broader the brand platform, the easier it is to extend into other categories.

BRAND EXTENSION PROCESS

Brand extension involves defining existing equities, then identifying new opportunity areas through business analysis and concept optimization.

Step 1: Confirm brand associations. Start by taking inventory of brand and category associations. What are the attributes and benefits? Lower rungs on the benefit hierarchy are a great place to start, as described earlier.

Figure 5.13 offers a sample list within the coffee category. Any of these ten brand associations may offer equity bridges for new business development.

Potential Coffee Category Extension Bridges

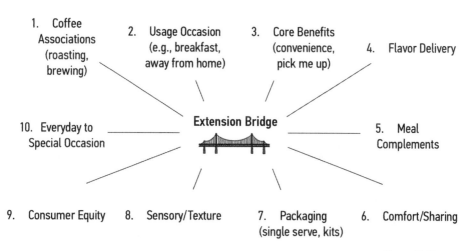

Figure 5.13

Step 2: Brainstorm and assess potential categories. Next, consider new categories and evaluate their size, growth, and profit potential. Closer-in opportunities might be new coffee flavors, coffee makers, instant coffee, or breakfast bars.

Further-out extensions might include desserts, soft drinks, and coffee-flavored ice cream at your grocer. Non-product extensions might include coffee delivery or self-service formats and new business models.

Step 3: Assess brand-category attractiveness. Drawing on steps 1 and 2, write simple one-sentence descriptions of each idea—linking the existing brand with the new category and unique benefit.

As a first pass, use business judgment, experience, and a 2 x 2 matrix to assess brand fit and business attractiveness (see figure 5.14).

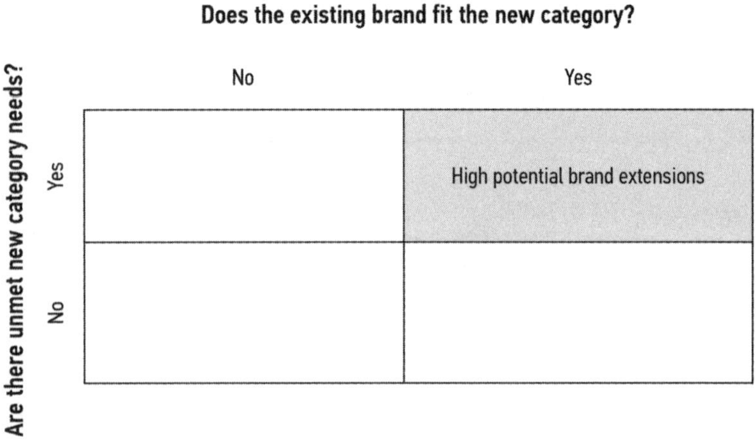

Does the existing brand fit the new category?

	No	Yes
Yes		High potential brand extensions
No		

Are there unmet new category needs?

Figure 5.14

On a scale of 1–10, does the extension idea logically fit with the brand? For example, like coffee, tea is brewed, so there is a potential bridge.

Then assess, 1–10, how satisfied customers are with the tea category on taste, quality, and other dimensions. Plot the results. If the brand fits and there is unmet demand, this may create an opening for stretching the brand.

Step 4: Conduct the concept optimization research (CORE) process. After assessing initial ideas, use focused ideation and concept iteration to identify and screen opportunities. See chapters 2, 6, and 8 for details, including the role of quantitative research to confirm idea strength.

Step 5: Develop an entry strategy and plan, including make-versus-buy decisions and portfolio management guidelines. Planning involves obtaining technical insights regarding how best to enter the new categories.

The risk of overextension

While selective brand extension makes sense, brands can be stretched too far, risking equity erosion and poor business performance.

Remember the Starbucks Via instant coffee line? Or perhaps you had a beer or glass of wine at one of the 400 or more stores participating in Starbucks' "Evening" program before it exited the concept in 2017.

Likewise, Nike has extended beyond running shoes to become a lifestyle brand, including apparel and equipment across multiple categories. They've also bridged to backpacks to store and carry shoes, balls, and equipment. But Nike binders sold at the corner drug store? This extension goes too far, though you can still find them on eBay.

Just because you *can* extend or license a brand, doesn't mean you *should*.

Brand and product managers can be reluctant to stretch brands, concerned about overextension. Lessen the risk by examining brand-category attractiveness through a structured approach. If you do this, significant, profitable growth is often just a brand extension away.

> There you have it—the four keys to brand management: establish the brand positioning, align the brand-customer experience, construct the brand architecture, and selectively extend the brand.

These four elements are vital to successfully marketing a business and driving growth. If you're not intentional about positioning your brand, somebody else will be, usually your competitor, so it's essential to manage the brand proactively.

MOVING FROM IDENTITY TO INNOVATION

"The world doesn't need another cookie." The client's comment was frustrating. Later, he'd add, "The nutrition and energy bar category is *way* too small and doesn't fit the brand." This was more concerning.

The client, a leading manufacturer of cookies and crackers, was looking to extend the brand into related snacking areas. This was in the mid-1990s, while Tim was working for another firm and also training as a weekend triathlete. The client didn't see the opportunity, but Tim saw it through a different lens.

Through weekend races, he had come across a new product category emerging on the circuit—energy bars. These first-generation products tasted awful—like a gritty paste made from nuts, leaves, and berries—but the samples were free and the benefits clear: real nutrition made from real ingredients.

The opportunity: What if you could blend the ultra-healthy ingredients of these early products with the form, convenience, and taste of a cookie?

Back at the office, the consulting team proposed a new concept idea—a line of nutritional bars made from healthy ingredients. The idea got shot down. The client thought their brand image was inconsistent with healthy eating (which it was), and the size of the energy bar category, around $100 million, was too small (also true).

The client was technically right on both counts. However, he saw things as they *were*, not how they *could be*. He looked at the brand from an identity perspective and failed to see the larger innovation opportunity.

Today, the energy bar category is over twenty times the size of what it was then and has crossed over to the mainstream. The rise of on-the-go snacking and healthy lifestyles, combined with improved taste and product delivery, has resulted in one of the few sizable food categories to emerge over the years, and the client missed out.

Insight and identity are critical marketing principles, but they're not enough. Combine them with the principle of innovation to get the full, magnifying effect of upstream marketing, as described next.

QUESTIONS TO CONSIDER

1. Is brand strategy a senior-level, boardroom topic in your organization?

2. Have you clearly established a relevant and differentiated brand positioning?

3. Are you making it easy for customers to buy from you, including aligning brand touchpoints with the customer decision process?

4. Do the various brands and products fit together in a way that makes it clear to customers what you offer?

PRINCIPLE 3

Innovation

INNOVATION

SO FAR, WE'VE COVERED TWO upstream marketing principles—insight and identity. Insight helps pinpoint growth opportunities, drawing on an organization's purpose and the customer demand framework. Identity uses value propositions and brand management to win against competitors.

With innovation, focus shifts to driving growth through a continuous stream of new business models, value propositions, products, and services.

Innovation is a broad topic that can take many forms. We define it this way: *Innovation is creating and capturing value in a new way.* Note two sub-points: *Creating and capturing value* links to value propositions. *In a new way* involves expanding beyond existing offerings to focus on new ways to grow. The framing questions to consider here are: how might we and what would have to be true?

Our research and experience indicate successful innovation requires two things. On the one hand, strategy, analytics, and process provide focus and promote efficiency. On the other hand, dynamic practices are needed to respond to new opportunities flexibly. The tricky part is that both stability and flexibility need to occur at the same time.

Chapter 6: Create, Test, and Learn (Strategy & Process) describes the need for structure and iteration. Successful innovation requires a planned, systematized approach infused with experimentation and problem solving. Strategic opportunity areas, focused ideation, concept iteration, and screening help ensure a consistent stream of innovation.

Chapter 7: Aim 'Em, Don't Tame 'Em (Creativity & Culture) stresses the social side of upstream marketing. The right people and a stimulating, supportive environment are vital for ideas to thrive.

In the end, strategy and culture feed one another. Executing a sound strategy strengthens culture, which in turn drives transformative growth.

CHAPTER 6

CREATE, TEST, AND LEARN (STRATEGY & PROCESS)

"Innovation distinguishes between a leader and a follower."

—Steve Jobs, *co-founder, chairman, and CEO of Apple, Inc.*

"Creativity is thinking up new things. Innovation is doing new things."

—Theodore Levitt, *professor, Harvard Business School*

"Few ideas work on the first try. Iteration is key to innovation."

—Sebastian Thrun, *innovator, entrepreneur, educator, and computer scientist*

WALT DISNEY SAID, "I ONLY hope that we don't lose sight of one thing—that it was all started by a mouse."[52] What began as a cartoon sketch on a twenty-minute train ride has morphed into the largest media company in the world, with assets in movies, television, publishing, resorts, and theme parks.

Beginning with animation, Disney has entered new markets and businesses across a host of products and services. Innovation occurs on multiple levels—both across businesses and within them. All the while, new products and brands are developed and extended to fuel growth.[53]

Figure 6.1, inspired by Walt's growth plans published in 1957, shows the strategic thinking behind them.

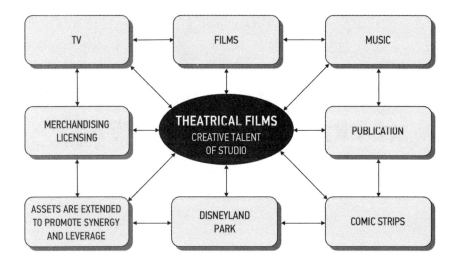

Figure 6.1

At the center is the creative talent of the studio, which creates the movies, from *Snow White and the Seven Dwarfs*, first shown in 1937, to the more recent *Frozen II*. Other assets extend from the center— Disneyland attractions, merchandise/licensing, and media, including TV, music, and publications. The arrows show how the assets relate to one another. In many cases, arrows go both ways: Assets infuse value ("feeds in raw material"), and value transfers back ("plugs Disneyland").[54]

Over time, Disney has found new ways to grow. Historically, assets were created in a film (*Toy Story*), then extended into other areas (Toy Story Mania, the theme park attraction). *Pirates of the Caribbean*, though, went in the opposite direction. It started as a Disneyland attraction and later became a blockbuster film franchise.

Innovation and brand extensions are also occurring at a faster rate. Take the animated film *Frozen,* released in 2013 as the fifty-third animated feature.

From there, it expanded to include a soundtrack, books, costumes, toys, an attraction, and the sequel film, *Frozen II,* launched six years later, in 2019. Compare this with the over fifty-year gap between the launch of *Mary Poppins* and *Mary Poppins Returns.*

Through it all, Disney employs upstream marketing brilliantly. It understands its target, designs winning value propositions and brands, and delivers a continuous stream of innovation.

Design thinking and concept iteration—storyboards, prototypes, and models—are used to develop and deliver magical experiences. Today, the company still employs many of the same principles and methods formulated by Mr. Disney all those years ago.

HOW DISNEY INNOVATES

Walt Disney said, "Of all the things I've done, the most vital is coordinating those who work with me and aiming their efforts at a certain goal."[55] Strategic focus—aiming the team—is crucial to the company's success.

The company's approach to innovation is in lockstep with upstream marketing. At The Walt Disney Company, deciding where to focus and how to win is a strategic resource allocation decision. While Imagineers and creative types receive a lot of attention, Disney's strategic planners, accountants, and technologists drive much of its success.[56] Though the company is one of the most creative in the world, it's also one of the most disciplined and strategically driven.

Disney uses where to play segmentation to define the playing field and tailor offerings. Within Disney Parks, for example, consider how a customer framework can help identify portfolio gaps to fill, as summarized here:

To Whom and For What? (Portfolio Gaps)	How to Win? (New Products/Offerings)
Teens (thrill seekers)	Tower of Terror/Guardians of the Galaxy, Star Wars Attractions
Cruisers (experience seekers)	Disney Cruise Lines
Seniors, spouses (R & R focused)	Golf resorts, Downtown Disney
Corporations (professional development)	Disney Institute, convention hotels

While Disney Parks performs well with certain segments—young families, in particular—it has struggled with other groups. Attracting thrill-seeking teens, for example, proved difficult in the early 1990s. Then, newly opened Universal Studios, with its roller coaster and thrill rides, cut into Disneyworld's attendance.

Disney could have created a taller, faster corkscrew roller coaster. While this may have been a hit with teens, it would have been incompatible with the "Disney Way" of delivering magical experiences.

Disney instead placed its how-to-win bet on the hugely successful Tower of Terror. Guardians of the Galaxy later replaced it (basically the same ride, with a new skin) as a Disney-owned film property. More recently, the company acquired other brand assets—Star Wars and Marvel, to name two—to fill the gap in target appeal.

The Dreamer, Realist, and Spoiler

The Walt Disney Company's approach to creativity and innovation has three parts, which stem from Walt's inspiration. According to Ollie Johnson, Disney animator, "There were actually three different Walts: the dreamer, the realist, and the spoiler. You never knew which one was coming into your meeting."[57] Embedded in Walt's creative approach are classic examples of create, test, and learn.

The dreamer comes up with new stuff without any filtering. Dreamers use blue-sky thinking and brainstorming to generate lots of ideas, without limits or judgment. Of course, many ideas at this stage are not that good. However, a spark of an idea can fuel other ideas. Bad ideas can become good ideas.

The realist takes the core ideas from the dreamer and makes them into something practical that works. This step involves prototyping concepts and testing them to see if they are even feasible. Concepts, in whatever form, are optimized to obtain feedback. The question here: How might we execute this vision?

The spoiler, or critic, shoots holes in the concepts. Focus shifts to the framing question: What would have to be true to succeed? The spoiler's job is to point out what's working and what's not and to feed that learning into the next round of iteration.

While "dreamer, realist, and spoiler" is classic Disney form, ideation (create), iteration (test), and screening (learn) is common across the profile companies.

Here's a look into how Google, Amazon and Apple create, test, and learn.

Google on Innovation[58]

Google views innovation as an ongoing process, rather than an episodic event. Google leadership uses a set of pillars to inform and support innovation across the organization:

Know the user involves getting out of the office, and into the field and talking to people—watching, listening and building customer empathy, then building on this insight. This is consistent with Google's overarching principle of focusing on the user, knowing that all else—including sales and profits—will follow.

Think 10x serves as an internal mantra to push the thinking far beyond incremental innovation. Simply put, Google believes breakthrough innovation occurs when trying to improve something by ten times instead of ten percent. This forces transformative thinking—resulting in big, bold and crazy ideas.

To support this, during brainstorming sessions, pictures are used to instill creative thinking and represent ideas. Concept statements are prepared, including short, six-word headlines designed to capture the essence of the idea. Also, as there's plenty of time to weed out bad ideas later, focus is on idea and concept generation, instead of concept screening. The goal is to move beyond "no but" to "yes and" thinking to build on and improve ideas.

Prototype. Design thinking and five-day design sprint sessions are used to create quick and dirty prototypes bringing ideas to life. Iteration is key. Ideas in the form of written concepts, mocked-up websites and other stimuli are developed, shared, and improved upon to gain insight.

Launch and learn. "Ship and iterate," "beta products," and "soft launch" are terms used to describe Google's approach to getting ideas out there quickly, obtaining market feedback and making on-going refinements.

> The concept of a "soft launch," borrows from the restaurant business in opening new establishments. Rather than a grand opening to the general public, a new cafe will have a few days or weeks when they invite only family and friends. This provides a chance to learn what works, iron out the kinks, and prepare for full-scale launch.

In Google's case, they'll launch software product 1.0 along with built-in feedback loops to address problems and expand functionality, followed quickly with version 1.1 and other iterations. This approach provides product development teams with real-time, real-world customer insight.

Amazon on Innovation

Amazon's "standard playbook" is to launch a product or service quickly, not make too big a deal of it, and spend almost nothing on marketing. Jeff Bezos said, "If you double the number of experiments you do per year, you're going to double your inventiveness." Amazon uses customer feedback to make adjustments or cut projects quickly.

Amazon uses an approach called "working backward" in developing new products. The process starts with the end customer rather than starting with an idea for a product and trying to bolt customers onto it.[59]

A product manager initiates the process by writing an "internal press release" directed to end customers and announcing the finished product and associated benefits. The press release draft centers on customer problems, and how the new product addresses them.

The product manager keeps iterating on the press release until critical benefits are identified and confirmed. Once the concept is approved and moves into development, the press release serves as a touchstone to achieve the confirmed customer benefits. Writing an early press release is beginning with the end in sight.

Apple's New Product Process

Apple's approach to innovation is codified in the Apple New Product Process (ANPP), which details every stage of the design process, including the various steps of development, who is responsible for delivering the final product, and when the product is expected to be completed. This includes weekly product reviews with Apple executives to assess progress.

Iteration is key throughout the design and development process. Products are built, tested, and reviewed, then the design team improves on them and they're built all over again. These cycles take four to six weeks at a time and may be run many times over a product's development life cycle.

Apple design teams are separated from the larger organization, both physically and organizationally. Design teams have their own organization structures and report directly to the executive team. This gives them freedom to focus on design rather than the day-to-day minutiae.

COMMON INNOVATION PRACTICES

A deep dive into the profile companies reveals that each has its own innovation strategy and process, which makes sense as they operate in different industries. Across the lot, they share the following five end-in-sight sub-principles:

- Focus innovation on strategic opportunity areas

- Generate ideas through creative problem solving

- Develop and optimize concepts iteratively

- Determine "What would have to be true?" for success

- Use a portfolio and pipeline approach to manage innovation

Let's explore each sub-principle in detail.

Focus Innovation on Strategic Opportunity Areas

As seen in the Disney, Google, Amazon, and Apple examples, innovation is more than "I have an idea." It needs to be aimed strategically, using a structured, disciplined approach. Replace the "fuzzy front end," as it's sometimes called, with clear direction (see figure 6.2).

Using Insight, Identity, and Innovation to Inform Upstream Marketing

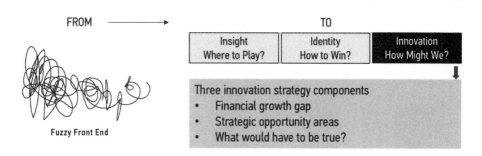

Figure 6.2

In establishing strategic direction, there are a few places to look for inspiration. Two we've talked about, insight and identity. The third ties to innovation, and consists of three interrelated elements—the financial growth gap, strategic opportunity areas, and what would have to be true business screening.

Financial growth gap defines how much revenue is needed beyond base business growth to achieve your goals. Are you looking to improve the business 10 percent, 100 percent, or like Google strives to, by ten times? Knowing this figure helps you strategically manage the innovation pipeline and portfolio.

In general, the larger the growth gap, the greater the need for innovation. Later in this chapter, we describe a range of innovation types, from incremental to transformational, that need to be strategically managed to help close the gap.

Consider that downstream marketing aligns with the base business, with upstream marketing required to fill the larger economic gap (see figure 6.3).

Innovation Growth Gap

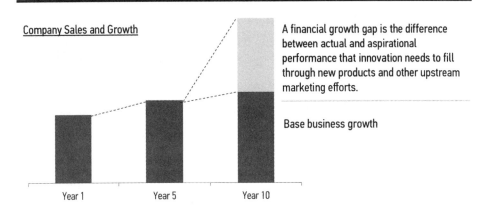

Company Sales and Growth

A financial growth gap is the difference between actual and aspirational performance that innovation needs to fill through new products and other upstream marketing efforts.

Base business growth

Year 1   Year 5   Year 10

Figure 6.3

Strategic opportunity areas (SOAs), as described in chapter 3, align with the growth gap and help pinpoint potential areas of growth to focus strategy, planning and customer research. A roll-up summary of individual SOAs should begin to fill the growth gap. If not, revise SOAs or add more to align with corporate growth objectives.

What would have to be true considers the business conditions necessary for success, including strategic, customer, financial, and operational screens, described later in this chapter.

These three elements—the growth gap, SOAs, and business screening—should come together in an upstream marketing plan and business case.

Exactly what to include in the planning template/business case depends on the industry, category, and SOA being considered. In creating Disneyland, for example, Harrison "Buzz" Price, who advised on operationalizing the park, created an entirely new set of business metrics in planning. Harrison said, "Over time, for Walt and his brother Roy, and those that followed, we invented an all-new vocabulary that is today the mathematical language of attraction development. It would include subjects like site analysis, concept development, market size, market penetration, attendance targets . . . and profitable economic performance."[60] Many of these metrics may apply to innovation planning within your own organization.

Once the strategy is in place, focused ideation is used to develop a range of benefit-based solutions to deliver on the opportunity.

Generate Ideas Through Creative Problem Solving

In truly innovative companies, free-flowing exchange of ideas happens naturally every day. Creativity extends beyond the marketing, strategy, and R&D departments. Brainstorming occurs outside the annual off-site planning session.

Still, there are times when dedicated problem-solving sessions make sense—for corporate planning, new products, and other efforts.

These problem-solving sessions can occur over a few hours to several days or longer, across two broad forms: focused ideation and design sprints. Both types focus on solving a particular problem within a specified period:

- Focused ideation is used to come up with an array of benefit-based solutions around a particular problem. Informed by deep insight and creative exercises, focused ideation sets the stage for meeting customer needs.

- A design sprint is a specific approach to ideation, often over five days, used to address business questions through design, prototyping, and testing ideas with customers.

These two methods work well alone or combined. Focused ideation takes a venture capitalist approach—develop and optimize a portfolio of concept areas.

Design sprints align with a startup mindset—iterate a single concept within a defined space. Combined, the methods spread risks and increase the chances of new business success.

Also, both methods rely on similar problem-solving techniques, defined as *convergent* and *divergent* thinking. Here is a typical ideation session agenda, made up of three parts.

Part 1. Define the problem, including "how might we" statements. Tee up the problem and share customer and market background. Present the to-whom, for-what framework, customer insight, and the benefit hierarchy. Cover market trends, technical insight, and initial hypotheses. List specific jobs to be done (or benefits sought), making sure to look at the job from the customer's perspective, not the company's.

Next, translate customer pain points, gain points, and jobs to be done into how-might-we questions. Rephrase problems into opportunities to encourage a free-flowing exchange of ideas without filtering.

For example, rather than relay the problem, "We're not selling enough baking mixes," restate the opportunity: "How might we deliver a specialty bakery experience at home?"

It's okay to have multiple how-might-we statements: "How might we deliver a healthy, portable breakfast ready in five minutes?" Or "How might we offer speed scratch, homemade cooking?" The deeper the insight, the better the questions, and the better the answer. Said another way, don't skimp on insights!

Wrap up Part 1 by sticky-dot-voting high-potential opportunity areas and ask two other questions: "Why should we address this?" and "What is stopping us?" Get it all out, then take stock of what's listed. This helps illuminate what to consider in ideating potential solutions.

Part 2. Conduct focused ideation exercises. Now, diverge and converge.

To diverge: After confirming the opportunities to focus on, table them, at least temporarily, to encourage breakthrough thinking.

When ideating too closely to defined problems, typically only incremental improvements result. Conversely, when broader perspectives are introduced, transformative solutions emerge.

Use creative exercises and projective techniques, time clocks, sticky note pads, and dot voting to facilitate the session. Here are some proven exercises.

PROVEN FACILITATED IDEATION EXERCISES

Brainwalking is a great exercise to surface an initial set of ideas. Most session participants have ideas they've been thinking about before the session itself. Put up large, self-stick flipchart paper around the room and assign one sheet to each participant. How might we solve this problem? Write the answers you came with on the sheet. Then, rotate a couple of times to your neighbors' stations to build on their ideas and create new ones. As a twist, write down the absolute *worst* idea, and then turn the bad idea into a good one.

Great Inventors is designed to bring in outside thinking. Brainstorm a list of inventors, entrepreneurs, and rule breakers, then list top-of-mind associations with those individuals. Working alone or in groups, create new concepts by viewing things through the inventors' eyes. How might Walt Disney, Steve Jobs, Jeff Bezos, or other creative thinkers solve the problem? How might we, through their eyes?

Picture Prompts uses outside stimuli to infuse new thinking—a picture is worth a thousand words. Participants peruse a wide range of magazines and "rip" pages of inspiration, then "rap" about why these caught their attention (no singing or dancing required). Photos, article headlines, and ads help unlock new ideas. Have team members create a print ad inspired by the scraps of headlines, photos, and copy.

Benefit Hooks consider customer needs, benefits sought, jobs to be done, and trigger words to stimulate creativity. First, list target benefits (speed, comfort, simplicity, etc.). Then, list things (nouns not verbs) that embody those benefits (speed = stopwatch, comfort = blanket, simplicity = fly swatter) including associated words. Finally, consider what's listed and brainstorm solutions to the identified problem. In removing yourself one or

continued

two steps from the problem—how might a fly swatter inspire a simple solution—breakthrough ideas emerge.

Metaphorical Baiting uses comparisons (e.g., time is money) to express and generate ideas. Comparing two unlike things based on something they have in common creates rich imagery to stimulate creative problem solving. Another example: Use other brands to inspire new ideas. We're the Uber/ Amazon/Airbnb/YETI of (insert category here).

Then, converge: After the ideation exercises, relate ideas to the job to be done and solve it. Use ideation templates to collect and organize the ideas for contrast and comparison. Figure 6.4 provides a sample worksheet.

Core Idea: How Might We?

		Illustration/Sketch
Headline/Core Benefit		
Target Problem/Needs Addressed		
Idea Description/ Proof Points/ Reasons to Believe • • •		
What would have to be true to be successful?		

Figure 6.4

Part 3. Prioritize the winners. Toward the end of the session, identify and converge on high-potential areas. Dot voting and the impact-effort matrix described in chapter 2 are great early ways to narrow the list of ideas. Other methods for screening ideas are described later in this chapter.

WHO ARE THE IDEAL SESSION ATTENDEES?

Carefully consider who to invite to ideation and design sprints, including a mix of three types of people:

Expansive thinkers. Open-minded individuals are vital to generating out-of-the-box thinking. Be careful with people who are apt to say, "We've already tried that." This is the idea generation phase and things change. There will be plenty of time to screen out bad ideas later.

Knowledgeable thinkers. People with in-depth insight into the business are good to include; cross-functional input infuses the session with varying points of view. Specialized insight is particularly valuable if the problem to solve has specific technical aspects, such as unique product characteristics and complex customer requirements.

Creative thinkers. The best sessions involve an element of humor and "playtime." While department heads may thrive on problem solving, if they'd rather not participate in the session, don't press them. Preferably, include them in the concept review process, as described next.

Be sure to use a combination of *individual* and *team* exercises, recognizing that people thrive in different environments.

Develop and Optimize Concepts Iteratively

After focused ideation and prioritization, put high-potential ideas into concept form—or tangible, testable propositions—to clarify thinking, obtain feedback, and iterate concepts. Use verbal concepts, visual imagery, and prototypes to "bring the concept to life" and seek input.

The concept optimization process itself is not linear but rather back-and-forth—learn as you go to get closer to the right solution, as shown in figure 6.5.

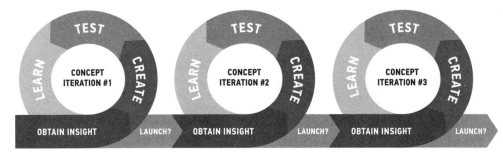

Figure 6.5

There are three iteration loops here, though there could be more or fewer, depending upon the business. What to optimize also varies (from concepts to minimum viable products) with timing ranging from several days to months or longer. The main thing? Use customer feedback to *shape* the answer, not just validate it afterward.

When optimizing concepts, expose one idea at a time to assess appeal and differentiation. Ask target customers, is the idea appealing—why or why not? What would it replace or add to? Use probing questions. What do you like about the idea? What don't you like, and how can it be improved? Across all areas, which concept is best, and why? If a concept is going to fail, have it fail fast and apply resources elsewhere.

A/B TESTING IN UPSTREAM MARKETING

The principles and practices described in *Upstream Marketing* work in online and offline environments. The idea of concept iteration, for example, can be automated through online A/B testing (also called split testing).

With A/B testing, two versions of a concept or a website are exposed to customers—a "control" version and a "test" version. For example, this could be one ad with two different headlines, with changes made based on test performance.

While A/B testing can be a powerful way to optimize offerings, this method has its limitations. For example, while A/B testing can indicate *which* concept is preferred, it does little to inform the *whys*—the insight behind the behavior.

Also, in evaluating concepts, it's often more effective to look beyond the "average" customer used in typical A/B trials to better understand customer segments.

Finally, it is useful to consider the long-term, cumulative effect of a *series of changes* instead of a single change.

When using A/B testing, artificial intelligence, and other automated methods, balance your findings with a qualitative understanding of the *whys* behind the preferences to obtain deeper insight.

CONCEPT OPTIMIZATION BENEFITS

The premise behind concept optimization is that it's easier and cheaper to develop, optimize, and test ideas in concept rather than final finished form. This test-and-learn approach offers several benefits:

More and better solutions emerge from exposing multiple concepts to customers. Locking in on one solution limits choice. Rather than optimize a single solution, cast a wide net using concepts as bait.

Customers can readily list problems and concerns but often find it difficult to identify solutions. Prototypes are easier for customers to react to and suggest refinements.

Concepts in unfinished form naturally invite interest. Often, the cruder the description, the better, at least initially. There's a natural desire to want to smooth out rough edges so respondents eagerly engage and provide feedback.

Concept development is more cost-effective than developing functioning products. Preparing a basic concept description requires maybe a day of focused ideation and another day of concept creation. Also, it's psychologically easier to kill a bad idea when sunk costs are a nonfactor.

When preparing concepts or prototypes, stress clarity and strategic benefits over creative appeal. While concepts should be neither boring nor bland, distill ideas down to their benefit essence and reason for being. Avoid "ad copy"—the turn of a phrase that can oversell a concept void of customer merit.

WHAT TO TEST AND OPTIMIZE

Stimuli to test and learn from depends on several factors, including cost and timing. The goal is to gain as much insight as possible relative to costs incurred. There is a range of testable propositions, as shown in figure 6.6.

Alternative Concept Testing Propositions				
Type	**Whiteboard Concepts**	**Visual Concepts**	**Physical Prototypes**	**Minimum Viable Products**
What is it?	Verbal descriptions, either on paper or a computer screen	Mock websites and marketing material to simulate end products in context	Physical models to bring the idea to life in a tangible way	Final "bare bones" products (with one or two main functions)
When used?	One-on-one research settings and surveys	Website /online settings and surveys	Feedback on physical, 3-D models	Proof of concept and next-level refinements
Cost to Create	Low	Low	Low to Medium	Low to High

Figure 6.6

In determining what to test, consider working your way from the left to the right, balancing quality feedback with keeping costs low. As certainty increases, invest in more involved testing methods.

Written whiteboard concepts are a great place to start. Distill ideas down to their benefit essence to assess whether the ideas address real needs.

From there, progress to visual concepts and physical prototypes. There's an added cost of next-level experiments but also richer insight.

Finally, consider minimum viable products (MVPs), creating and then testing the first form of a functioning product. Said another way, launch and learn.

The stimuli to use depends on the industry and product category. Going with an MVP or "soft launch" makes sense for software, services, and other sectors where iterations are cost-effective. MVPs, though, may be impractical for other categories. A commitment to iteration is more important than what's tested. The real value is in obtaining insight to get closer to the end solution.

CREATE, TEST, AND LEARN AT EQUIBRAND

Numerous methods exist to work backward and test early business ideas using concept statements and other prototypes. With EquiBrand engagements, we almost always begin with simple, benefit-based whiteboard concepts. They're inexpensive to produce, are easy for customers to react to, and help get the organization "on the same page." Next, we favor website prototypes, adding visual interest and look-feel detail.

In creating *Upstream Marketing*, in addition to concept optimization, we used the following mini tests to assess market appeal and improve the end product:

- Created a simple *Upstream Marketing* website, including an initial draft of chapter 1. This clarified our thinking and established an initial online presence to track website traffic.

- Generated a book mock-up (prior to finishing the manuscript), shown on the website along with a preorder form for email capture. Potential readers could select from "I'm interested in reading an advance copy of the book" or "Notify me when the book is published."

continued

- Set up Google Alerts so that whenever the words "upstream marketing" appeared in a new article, website, or news release, we were notified by email. This free detection service allowed us to track customer and competitive activity.

- Used Google Trends to chart the popularity of "upstream marketing," including graphs that compared search volume over time with other terms.

- Wrote and placed alternative "upstream marketing" Google pay-per-click ads to research and optimize the title and subtitle, through A/B ad conversion.

- Prepared advance reader copies and sought advice and feedback from professional contacts and prior clients on key themes and company examples.

Determine "What Would Have to Be True?" for Success

Imagine the discussion Nike executives had in 1984 deciding whether to sign Michael Jordan out of North Carolina to a seven-year, $6.3 million contract.[61] What proof did company leaders have that the investment would pay out? Zero.

Fortunately, Nike's culture promotes innovation and healthy risk taking. It's one of *just do it* rather than *just prove it*. Today, the Jordan brand generates billions in sales annually for Nike, hitting its first $1 billion quarter in 2019.

Of course, Nike protected its downside through an out clause: If Jordan didn't sell $4 million worth of shoes by the third year, Nike could cancel the deal.[62]

Nike established this threshold based on certain "what would have to be true" assumptions. They needed to ensure investing in the rising star wasn't a complete bust. As it was, Nike sold $70 million worth of Air Jordans in the first two months of 1985, and the rest is, well, history.

A CAUTION AGAINST "PROVE IT" AND "SHOW ME THE MONEY"

The death knell of innovation is "Prove it." Many executives want proof that a new business idea will achieve an economic payback before investing in it.

In most cases, though, the proof won't come right away. So, companies never pull the trigger. They never realize the benefits of upstream marketing. They stagnate and lose.

While desired, financial forecasting too early in upstream planning is risky for a couple of reasons. First, truly new ideas have never been done before, so no real data exists regarding their potential. Absent historical data, analysis paralysis sets in—creating a business case becomes a project in itself.

Second, predicted numbers provide a false sense of security. Most projections will be wrong, yet creating them makes them seem more real than they are.

MINI CASE EXAMPLE

Be cautious about total addressable market (TAM) projections and spreadsheet calculations. These can be sensitive to minor changes in assumptions. We worked with a Silicon Valley software startup that used an elaborate formula to calculate market potential. Changing one number in the spreadsheet, from a 10 percent market share projection to 20 percent, substantially altered the forecast.

Nothing changed in the company's strategy, other than plugging in this one number. Yet the company—at least on paper—went from losing money to being wildly profitable within twelve months.

While many investment decisions require financial pro formas, treat upstream forecasts differently. Rather than seek a wild guess on economic potential, use a test-and-learn approach, periodically asking: What needs to be proven to proceed?

WHAT WOULD HAVE TO BE TRUE?

Our team first heard this question while working on a growth strategy project for the leading home services company. The client executive, a former McKinsey partner, kept asking, "What would have to be true?" when assessing alternatives.

It seemed like an odd way to phrase a question, and a bit confusing, but we figured the language was intentional.

Like other upstream marketing tools, this question requires that you begin with the end in sight and think through ahead of time what's needed to succeed.

Go upstream and assess the situation: What are the success parameters—building a sales force, securing retail placement, or commanding a specific price? Once you know what would have to be true, use mini tests and trials to either prove or disprove your hypotheses.

By way of example, let's revisit the lemonade stand case from chapter 3. Say you've done some research and created a plan to build the stand in the desert. Customers want the product, so it clears that hurdle. For the venture to succeed, though, it requires serving an average of fifty customers a day, each spending $5. Is it true you can charge that amount?

Also, the concept requires solar energy to power operations. Can this be delivered operationally? What else would need to be proven before proceeding with the idea? Screening ideas with questions like these is a critical aspect of strategy development.

FOUR SCREENING AREAS

The impact-effort matrix (described in chapter 3) is a useful starting point for assessing growth potential. As business ideas take shape, though, you'll want to apply greater rigor in evaluating ideas. Approach the analysis from four perspectives—strategic, customer, financial, and operational—to cover all bases.

These same four screening areas can be used at different times in prioritizing opportunities: initially in determining where to play, and then again in screening how-to-win concepts.

Figure 6.7 lists the four business screens on the left side. At the top are potential concept areas (labeled A, B, C, and D). Each concept is evaluated against each screen.

What would have to be true?					
Screen	Sample Criteria	A	B	C	D...
Strategic	• Fit with company mission, vision, strategy	◖	◕	◖	◕
Customer	• Customer need intensity (relevance) • Uniqueness (differentiation)				
Financial	• Relative size of opportunity (metrics TBD)				
Operational	• Degree of business efficiency; operational fit and leverage				

Figure 6.7

In evaluating concepts, use shaded circles to delineate high-to-low rankings across screening areas. These circles (sometimes called Harvey balls, named after the Booz Allen Hamilton consultant who created them) can add an element of structure and fun to the process of weeding out bad ideas.

At the early stages, compare and rank strategic opportunities based primarily on experience and judgment. Closer to launch, strive for more objective and quantifiable measures in refining the offering. Assess concepts early and often to weed out bad ideas and improve existing ones.

During early screening of strategic opportunity areas, evaluate *relative* rather than *absolute* measures. Instead of providing a tight forecast number—this opportunity is worth X dollars—ask, which alternative is best?

Later on, use quantitative research to size the market for concepts that pass initial screens. You can then measure concepts against a database of earlier ideas to determine potential success rates.

ENGAGE EXECUTIVES EARLY AND OFTEN

Upstream marketing can have a huge impact on a company's future direction, so it pays to involve senior stakeholders early in strategy development.

Unfortunately, many lower level managers wait too long to involve top executives, seeking "buy-in" after the slide deck has been prepared, polished and presented.

This is a bad approach, as it ignores executives' experience and broad perspective. Also, it can signal you don't value their contribution.

Walt Disney, Steve Jobs and Jeff Bezos are notorious "control enthusiasts," and it's hard to argue with their success. The reality? Most executives want to be involved in strategy formation. So, seek their alignment, feedback and contribution as early and often as you can.

After assessing ideas, it's time to put them into the innovation portfolio and pipeline, as described next.

Use a Portfolio and Pipeline Approach to Manage Innovation

It's been a while since consumers literally camped out overnight at an Apple store to purchase the latest iPhone. And while Apple launch events still generate buzz, the real magic occurs in how Apple strategically manages its innovation development cycle. Apple ensures a steady release of products, resulting from its planned portfolio and pipeline approaches.

Similarly, Google carefully manages its innovation portfolio by employing a careful product strategy, including the use of its 70/20/10 model.

GOOGLE ON ITS USE OF THE 70/20/10 MODEL

We're firm believers in a concept first introduced in the early days of Google: the 70/20/10 model. Simply put, it means:

- 70 percent of our projects are *dedicated* to our core business

- 20 percent of our projects are *related* to our core business

- 10 percent of our projects are *unrelated* to our core business

- We [Google] have a few goals in mind here. One is that this model is a helpful way to allocate resources as we think about the big picture of our business each year. It keeps the focus on core needs while also encouraging a healthy stretch into new and related areas.

Just as importantly, the 70/20/10 model supports a culture of "yes" rather than "no." It promotes what-if, out-of-the-box thinking. This positive framework feeds our core business while also encouraging new ideas and big dreams that can become huge wins for the company—those 10x moonshots we were talking about earlier. In the long run, a few of those unrelated 10 percent ideas will turn into core businesses that become part of the 70 percent. And that's good for business and the bottom line.[63]

Best practice companies take both a pipeline and portfolio view of their innovation, ensuring a consistent stream of new product ideas, including a mix of incremental and transformational ones over time. This strategic, balanced approach allows them to develop and manage ideas of all sizes and at various stages of development.

This approach also conditions customers and internal team members to expect a continual stream of innovation. It's a virtuous cycle—insight-led innovation enhances a company's identity. The upstream marketing principles build upon and reinforce each other, expanding a company's branded assets (see figure 6.8.)

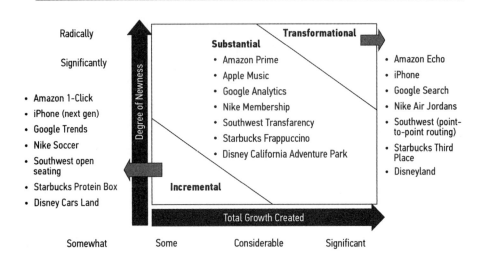

Figure 6.8

Consider the three broad types of innovation, as shown above:

1. **Incremental innovation** provides continuous improvement to a company's core business and existing capabilities in the short term.

2. **Substantial innovation** extends a company's business and core capabilities to new customers, markets, or targets.

3. **Transformational innovation** establishes new capabilities and new business, responding to disruptive opportunities.

Given business requirements and associated risk, a balance of incremental and transformational "big ideas" is necessary. Having multiple irons in the fire helps diversify risk and ensure a continuous stream of innovation over time.

In managing growth, be mindful that transformative innovation requires different focus, tools, and goals from the core business. This has organizational implications, as will be discussed in the next chapter.

Also, upstream marketing portfolio planning should be a top-down and bottom-up process. The executive team outlines broader business goals consistent with the corporate strategy. Individual SOA team leaders should then own their work and update executives on project goals, plans, and business case details to ensure alignment.

While the planning process should anchor annually to ensure a corporate-wide view, hold monthly meetings to track SOA progress. Markets are dynamic, so consider strategy as a journey. Track and monitor the portfolio and pipeline of upstream initiatives on a rolling basis, and adjust accordingly. Encourage continuous executive engagement on strategy using a four-page planning template, as described in chapter 8.

Of course, you don't arrive at a well-managed innovation portfolio overnight. It takes commitment to numerous things—identifying strategic opportunity areas, using creative problem solving to develop and optimize concepts, and determining success conditions.

STRATEGY AND PROCESS MEETS CREATIVITY AND CULTURE

Each profile company has well-honed innovation processes. But that's only half the equation. The counterbalance to process discipline is creativity and culture.

Apple's Steve Jobs talked about the balance this way: "Apple is a very disciplined company, and we have great processes. But that's not what it's about. Process makes you more efficient. But innovation comes from people meeting up in the hallways or calling each other at 10:30 at night with a new idea, or because they realized something that shoots holes in how we've been thinking about a problem. It's ad hoc meetings of six people called by someone who thinks he has figured out the coolest new thing ever and who wants to know what other people think of his idea."[64]

Jeff Bezos held similar concerns about being overly dependent on process, saying, "The process is not the thing. It's always worth asking, do we own the process, or does the process own us?"[65]

Some companies view culture as the "soft stuff" that doesn't matter. However, creativity and culture (as described in the next chapter) are the aspects that most distinguish world-class innovators.

QUESTIONS TO CONSIDER

1. Is there an innovation strategy that aligns with the corporate strategy and promotes a continuous stream of new products?

2. Does a confirmed list of strategic opportunity areas exist to focus the organization?

3. Is there internal commitment to experimentation and concept iteration as ways to achieve growth?

CHAPTER 7

AIM 'EM, DON'T TAME 'EM (CREATIVITY & CULTURE)

"Everybody believes in innovation until they see it.
Then they think, "Oh, no; that'll never work. It's too different."
—**Nolan Bushnell,** *entrepreneur and engineer, Atari and Chuck E. Cheese*

"When it comes to innovation, the candid organization will
outperform the nice one every time."
—**Gary Pisano,** *professor, Harvard Business School*

"Culture eats strategy for breakfast."
—**Peter F. Drucker,** *author,* The Practice of Management

THERE IS AN INSIDE JOKE at The Walt Disney Company that goes like this:

> **Question:** How many Disney Imagineers does it take to screw in a light bulb?
>
> **Answer:** Does it have to be a light bulb?[66]

The answer to this question speaks volumes about the culture of creativity that permeates Disney and the other profile companies.

While best practice innovators focus on business results, they also emphasize creativity and culture that is anything but paint by numbers. They are driven by facts, figures, and process discipline, but also embrace creativity, develop culture, and challenge conventional thinking.

Of course, the best innovation strategy and process in the world won't make a difference if the culture isn't there to drive it. And not just any culture. The culture needs to recognize and support the paradoxical nature of growth and innovation—the need to *aim 'em, don't tame 'em*—which exists on multiple levels.

At the highest level, strategy, analytics, and process discipline need to balance with creativity and flexibility. The company should be strategically aimed, but not so tamed that it loses its agility.

Aim 'em, don't tame 'em also applies to the people highly innovative companies hire. Eric Schmidt, Google's former chief executive, and Jonathan Rosenberg, a former senior product manager, wrote *How Google Works*, which refers to "smart creatives"[67] as the primary people-asset around which to build teams, companies, and corporate cultures.

Smart creatives, the authors write, are impatient, outspoken risk takers, "combining technical depth with business savvy and creative flair."

A challenge with smart creatives, the authors note, is providing an environment where they can thrive: "Their common characteristic is that they work hard and are willing to question the status quo and attack things differently. This is why they can have such an impact. It is also why they are uniquely difficult to manage, especially under old models, because no matter how hard you try, you can't tell people like that how to think. If you can't tell someone how to think, then you have to learn to manage the environment where they think. And make it a place where they want to come every day."[68] Embedded in this assessment is the notion of aiming but not taming smart creatives.

Finally, aim 'em, don't tame 'em needs to influence the shared values, attitudes, beliefs, and behaviors that determine how employees interact.

Harvard Business School professor Gary Pisano talks about the often-misunderstood hard truths of innovative cultures this way: "The fun and easy-to-like aspects of innovation need to be counterbalanced by some tougher and frankly less fun behaviors. A tolerance for failure requires an intolerance for incompetence. A willingness to experiment requires rigorous discipline. Psychological safety requires comfort with brutal candor. Collaboration must be balanced with individual accountability. And flatness requires strong leadership."[69]

Innovative cultures are paradoxical. The lines between these "aim 'em, don't tame 'em" points are thin, and managing these nuances can be the difference between innovation success and failure.

CULTURE AT THE PROFILE COMPANIES

Do an online search on any of the profile companies, and you'll get a sense of their culture and values—customer-centricity, innovation, speed, and creativity.

Many companies, though, pepper their corporate statements with similar words. What, then, distinguishes truly innovative companies from those that would only like to be? Hint: It's not a plaque on the wall.

One of the more exciting aspects of our work at EquiBrand is experiencing firsthand the cultures of our client companies.

This experience lets us see what goes on inside the company's boardroom on a couple of levels.

First, how does the company operate, and what does it value? What is the company's cultural style—is it friendly, combative, or somewhere in between? Are employees engaged, energized, and happy to be there? Or do they look scared, tired, or burned out?

Second, how is the boardroom set up *literally*? What is the room like, who sits where, and how are meetings conducted? Is there a poster on the wall detailing the company's mission, vision, and value statements? A poster can be a red flag for an unengaged company.

Our research and experience have identified a distinct set of cultural best practices that successful companies share in their upstream efforts. Let's examine a few profile companies in isolation, pulling from a diverse set of corporate statements, and then distill the findings into a universal set of cultural success principles.

Amazon's Culture and Values

Amazon casts its values as "leadership principles," which the company considers in solving problems and charting growth. These fourteen principles, listed on the company's website, are designed to work together, balancing accountability, efficiency, risk taking, and results.

AMAZON'S LEADERSHIP PRINCIPLES[70]

1. Customer Obsession
2. Ownership
3. Invent and Simplify
4. Are Right, A Lot
5. Learn and Be Curious
6. Hire and Develop the Best
7. Insist on the Highest Standards
8. Think Big
9. Bias for Action
10. Frugality
11. Earn Trust
12. Dive Deep
13. Have Backbone; Disagree and Commit
14. Deliver Results

Each of the leadership principles (or LPs as they're called at Amazon) deliver on the principles and practices of upstream marketing. Let's look at the ten that are particularly relevant.

Customer Obsession ties to Amazon's maniacal focus on the customer. Amazon starts with the customer, by working backward and ends with the customer, in keeping their trust. Leaders pay attention to competitors but obsess over customers.

Ownership stresses the need to think long term and not sacrifice future value for short-term results. This principle brings to mind the 2 x 2 high-low/urgent-important time management matrix as a way to prioritize long-term strategy and planning.

Invent and Simplify challenges leaders to find ways to innovate by reducing friction. Many of Amazon's top innovations—1-Click ordering and selling used items right next to new items on the same webpages—are simple, non-technical solutions to address customer friction points. This LP is consistent with the "jobs to be done" approach to innovation.

Learn and Be Curious advocates that leaders be curious about new possibilities and act to explore them. The best sources of insight and inspiration? See the first LP, *Customer Obsession.*

Think Big is all about creating and communicating a bold direction that inspires results. Thinking small, by contrast, is a self-fulfilling prophecy. Leaders think differently and uncover new ways to serve customers.

Bias for Action recognizes that speed matters. Amazon values calculated risk taking and a launch-and-learn approach, recognizing that many decisions and actions do not require extensive study and are often reversible.

Frugality means doing more with less. Think the Pareto principle and Parkinson's law combined. Constraints breed resourcefulness, self-sufficiency, and innovation.

Dive Deep encourages leaders to operate at all levels, stay involved in the details, audit frequently, and be skeptical when metrics and anecdotes differ.

Have Backbone; Disagree and Commit advocates that leaders respectfully challenge decisions even when they disagree. Leaders have conviction, are candid, and do not compromise just to be nice. Once a decision is determined, however, they commit wholly.

Deliver Results rounds out leadership principles and talks about focusing on key inputs, delivering them with the right quality and in a timely fashion. Setbacks will be inevitable, though leaders rise to the occasion and never settle.

Taken as a whole, Amazon's culture is performance-focused and customer-driven and proves internal values don't need to be "warm and fuzzy" to be effective. While Amazon has been criticized for a culture many perceive as impersonal and combative, this critique doesn't seem to bother Jeff Bezos, who talks about leadership and culture this way: "To get something new done, you have to be stubborn and focused, to the point that others might find unreasonable."[71]

While "stubborn, focused, and unreasonable" may not be traits described in a leadership textbook, these "less fun" aspects are precisely the corporate values that fuel innovation at Amazon.

Nike's Culture and Values

Nike's brand is synonymous with innovation, and the company is unique among profile companies in that it explicitly states innovation in its mission statement:

> "To bring inspiration and innovation to every athlete* in the world.
> *If you have a body, you are an athlete."[72]

Nike's mission cleverly incorporates its core marketing target ("to every athlete") and consumption target ("if you have a body, you're an athlete").

Innovation is a core value at Nike, informed by deep insight. Nike describes in its recruitment material how it works with the world's best athletes to obtain and leverage their views.

"To us, innovation is about elevating human potential. We obsess over the needs of the world's best athletes, using their insights to create products that are beautiful and useful. To make big leaps, we take big risks. Incremental change won't get us to where we want to go fast enough. We unite diverse perspectives—scientists and shoe designers, coders and quarterbacks—to share knowledge of the body in motion."[73]

Comparing Nike's mission, vision, and values to Amazon's leadership principles shows some similarities and differences.

Nike's culture is both competitive, like Amazon's, and team oriented. This trait makes sense as Nike's culture stems from its employees—many of whom are current or former athletes—as well as the athletes who endorse Nike products.

While much of Amazon's culture stems from Jeff Bezos, Nike cofounder and chairman Phil Knight, unassuming and introverted by nature, points out other influences: "Nike's culture is not the same as me. I've said before that Nike's culture is young and irreverent and I'm neither. It comes from the people. I have fingerprints on it but I didn't dictate it at all. But [we've learned things] from athletes that we've dealt with over the years, yes. We are in a very competitive industry and watching their reaction to competition and understanding the losses that have to come with the wins."[74]

Knight goes on to reference the Michael Jordan TV ad, dubbed "Failure": "I've missed more than nine thousand shots in my career. I've lost almost three hundred games. Twenty-six times, I've been trusted to take the game-winning shot and missed. I've failed over and over and over again in my life. And that is why I succeed."[75]

The next three companies profiled—Southwest, Starbucks, and Walt Disney—are similar in a couple of ways. As service-based businesses, much of the brand experience is delivered through their front-line people—flight attendants, partners, and attraction cast members. Also, to ensure they hire the best, corporate and brand-building efforts are designed to attract both employees and end customers.

Southwest's Culture and Values[76]

No discussion of culture would be complete without profiling Southwest. The company is known for its "fun-LUVing" attitude, as well as the importance it puts on culture in hiring and company operations. Here's an overview of Southwest's corporate statements.

Southwest's purpose: Connect people to what's important in their lives through friendly, reliable, and low-cost air travel.

Southwest's vision: To be the world's most loved, most efficient, and most profitable airline.

Southwest's company promise: To provide a stable work environment with equal opportunity for learning and personal growth. Employees are provided the same concern, respect, and caring attitude that they are expected to share externally with every Southwest Customer.

SOUTHWEST'S EMPLOYEE PROMISE: TO FOCUS ON DEMONSTRATING

1. Warrior Spirit by striving to be my best and never giving up;

2. Servant's Heart by delivering Legendary Customer Service and treating others with respect; and

3. Fun-LUVing Attitude by not taking myself too seriously and embracing my Southwest Family.

Southwest views its hiring practices as vital to the company's success. Rather than try to mold employees a certain way, Southwest recruits employees who are engaged from the start.

The company hires not for skill, but rather for three corporate values. Southwest then links these values to performance appraisals, including 360-degree reviews, where employees get rated for their warrior spirit, servant's heart, and fun-loving attitude.

While there is no mention of innovation in Southwest's values, the company advocates an upstream approach to people management: If you treat employees well, they'll find unique, creative ways to solve problems and deliver outstanding service.

CUSTOMER INSIGHT TIP

The same insight gathering techniques used with customers can work equally well with employees. Qualitative and quantitative research methods, including employee concept iteration and engagement surveys, can be used to ensure development, alignment, and delivery of brand and cultural values. This includes obtaining internal feedback on human resources policies and programs before implementing them.

Starbucks' Culture and Values

Establishing a culture that nurtures talent and supports innovation is not easy. But it can be done. Howard Schultz describes it this way: "People have come to me over the years and said to me: 'I admire the culture of Starbucks. Can you come give a speech and help us turn our culture around?' I wish it were that easy. Turning a culture around is very difficult to do because it's based on a series of many, many decisions, and the organization is framed by those decisions."[77]

Schultz understands that there are as many cultures as there are

companies, and each one is unique, based on the organization it supports. Starbucks' mission and values go far beyond coffee to celebrate
human connection and experience. Let's take a look.

> Starbucks' mission is to inspire and nurture the human spirit—one person,
> one cup, and one neighborhood at a time.

Starbucks values support the mission as follows:

> With our partners, our coffee, and our customers at our core, we live these
> values:[78]
>
> • Creating a culture of warmth and belonging, where everyone is
>   welcome.
>
> • Acting with courage, challenging the status quo, and finding new ways
>   to grow our company and each other.
>
> • Being present, connecting with transparency, dignity, and respect.
>
> • Delivering our very best in all we do, holding ourselves accountable for
>   results.
>
> We are performance-driven, through the lens of humanity.

Starbucks' last value statement—*We are performance-driven, through
the lens of humanity*—is not far from Google's *You can make money without doing evil* (and its original mantra, *Don't be evil*). Starbucks, though,
says it in a more uplifting way. Words matter in crafting corporate statements so take care in creating them.

Disney's Culture and Values

The Walt Disney Company's corporate statements are notable in how
they've changed over time. Walt described the company's purpose as "To

make people happy." Now? "The mission of The Walt Disney Company is to entertain, inform, and inspire people around the globe through the power of unparalleled storytelling, reflecting the iconic brands, creative minds, and innovative technologies that make ours the world's premier entertainment company."[79] Sounds like it was written by the corporate planning department, doesn't it? While the statement is descriptive, it lacks the simplicity and inspiration of "make people happy."

As is often the case, corporate statements can get watered down as companies expand into multiple products and markets.

In this case, business narratives, brand story, positioning, and messaging can play a more meaningful role. These statements serve as both an anchor and a beacon to guide decision making consistent with corporate-level aspirations.

Here, for example, is a listing of "Mickey's Ten Commandments" tied to Disney's Imagineering group. In 1991, Marty Sklar (then-president of Imagineering) presented ten commandments attributed to Mickey Steinberg.

MICKEY'S TEN COMMANDMENTS[80]

1. Know your audience

2. Wear your guests' shoes (don't forget the human factors; try to experience the parks from the guests' point of view)

3. Organize the flow of people and ideas (ensure experiences tell a story that is organized and logically laid out)

4. Create a "visual magnet"

5. Communicate with visual literacy (use a dominant color or shape or building to reinforce a theme)

6. Avoid overload—create turn-ons (do not offer too much detailed information)

continued

7. Tell one story at a time (put one "big idea" in each show so guests leave with a clear understanding of the theme)

8. Avoid contradictions—maintain identity (avoid irrelevant or contradicting elements; make sure the audience has a clear idea of what is being said)

9. For every ounce of treatment, provide a ton of treat (take advantage of the distinction of the theme park, which is that it encourages active participation, compared to passive entertainment)

10. Keep it up (do not become complacent or allow things to run down)

Note two things. First, how "Disney-like" the commandments are. While at a lower level than corporate statements, the Imagineering group's values are consistent with what you'd expect from The Walt Disney Company and appear to still hold today. Second, how the ten commandments align with the upstream marketing principles and best practices.

Read down the list. The first two commandments speak to the principle of insight—know your audience and wear your guests' shoes. Next are a series of identity-related directives—tell a story, reinforce a theme, maintain identity, and so on. The list ends with the principle of innovation—keep it up and avoid complacency.

COMMON INNOVATIVE CULTURES

Many companies have a culture that supports innovation. Far fewer have innovation embedded in their corporate DNA. A systematic review of the seven best practice marketers yields seven distinct cultures. Across all profile companies, though, five common cultural themes emerge:

• Create an aspirational identity to guide the organization

• Establish cultural values that support innovation

- Hire the right people and the right mix of people
- Establish practices to support innovation
- Organize for and commit to innovation

Innovative cultures start with an aspirational philosophy that then quickly grounds smart, creative people in accountability for the organization's goals, strategies, and stakeholder commitments. These lessons learned are described next.

Create an Aspirational Identity to Guide the Organization.

A defining trait of each profile company is an aspirational purpose and brand to focus and stretch the organization. They build a deep and shared understanding of the customer and brand and generally know where they're headed and how to get there.

Amazon set out to be earth's most customer-centric company. Google seeks to organize the world's information and make it universally accessible and usable. Starbucks wants to inspire and nurture the human spirit—one person, one cup, and one neighborhood at a time.

Establishing an organization's purpose is mostly an internal effort, though with obvious identity implications. Once the purpose is defined, company leaders need to consistently and publicly communicate it.

Starting at the top, executives need to "walk the talk"—live the culture and provide superior vision and direction. These actions reinforce the organization's values, which in turn directs how employees operate.

Establish Cultural Values That Support Innovation.

A company's values are the core of its culture. Call them values, leadership principles, or maxims—they orient employees' everyday actions to be consistent with the desired culture.

Value statements, though, are not platitudes. You cannot borrow a list from one company, erase the name on top, and replace it with another.

Amazon's leadership principles scream Amazon, including a focus on speed, efficiency, and expansion. Nike's values elevate athleticism, innovation, and competition. Starbucks' "warm and belonging" values differ from the more competitive ones of Amazon, Nike, and other companies.

Despite individual company differences, our research has identified five corporate values all intentionally created and shared by the profile companies. These values relate to: customer obsession, a growth mindset, thinking big, idea meritocracy, and the role of failure in innovation. Here are the details:

FIVE CORE INNOVATION VALUES

Value 1: Focus on and obsess about the customer.

By now, the importance of the end customer to growth strategy should be evident. The profile companies place the customer at the center of their innovation efforts. Here's a recap:

- "Leaders start with the customer and work backward," is Amazon's first leadership principle.

- Topping the list of Google's "Ten things we know to be true" is "Focus on the user, and all else will follow."

- "Everything we do starts with the consumer," says former Nike CEO, Mark Parker. "It's our obsession with serving the consumer that sharpens our focus and drives our growth."[81]

Still, it's surprising how many companies, including some of our clients, focus on targets other than the end consumer. Non-customer targets include internal team members ("What will the executives think?"), channel members

("We need to get retailers to stock it first"), or Wall Street ("We need to make our quarterly numbers"). Focusing on the end customer requires more than a head nod and must include the entire organization, from the corner office to customer service and frontline workers.

Value 2: Employ a growth mindset.

Embracing a growth mindset allows innovators to see spaces others do not. Here's a brief story to illustrate.

Two shoe sales representatives from competing companies visit the deep jungle in search of new customers.

The first sales rep returns and reports to his boss: "There's no market for us here. Nobody wears shoes."

The second sales rep returns and reports to his boss: "There's a huge market for us here. Nobody wears shoes!"

This simple story says a lot about the importance of a growth mindset. It's the same situation, yet two people draw very different conclusions. Some see the glass as half full, others as half empty. The most effective innovators? They create opportunities where others don't. It's fundamental to their culture.

Eric Schmidt, Google's former CEO, describes it this way: "The characteristic of great innovators and great companies is they see a space that others do not. They don't just listen to what people tell them; they actually invent something new, something that you didn't know you needed, but the moment you see it you say, I must have it."[82]

Value 3: Think big (but start small and learn fast).

Of course, in the shoe story here, it's conceivable that there is a market for footwear despite the fact that nobody wears shoes. However, it would be premature for the footwear company to build a new manufacturing plant in or near the jungle. "If you build it, they will come," is a wish, not a strategy.

So, experiment to learn, using the consumer as the tiebreaker for how to proceed. In the footwear example, maybe conduct an ethnographic study and seed the market with different shoe samples. Create a series of prototypes that replicate the feeling of not wearing shoes at all. Then, gradually expose other prototypes with greater construction and support. (This gives a whole new meaning to the expression, "walk before you run.")

continued

Value 4: Ensure the best ideas win.

The best innovations come from the best ideas, which in turn come from a culture where the best ideas win. When the organization is optimized for innovation, good ideas surface easily and circulate quickly within it.

Great ideas can come from anywhere—the CEO, division leader, summer intern, or end consumer. In our consulting work, some of the best ideas come from people at lower levels or new to the organization. This idea source is not surprising. Newer employees aren't tied to the past and are often closer to the end customer, so they can readily spot problems and potential solutions.

Here's the issue: Many improvement ideas only surface during one-on-one interviews, and only after we guarantee confidentiality. New employees can be hesitant to speak out, especially when suggesting new ways of doing things, for fear of repercussions.

Promoting a culture where the best ideas win means encouraging all team members to challenge conventional thinking without fear. Everyone's thoughts should be heard, with the best ideas rewarded. It also means recognizing the role of failure in innovation, as discussed next.

Value 5: Recognize productive failures.

It's easy to advocate for innovation when things go well. In reality, most new ventures, new business models, and new products do not succeed. The real test of an innovation culture is what happens when things fail, as they will most of the time.

According to Amazon's Jeff Bezos, "Failure comes part and parcel with invention. It's not optional. We understand that and believe in failing early and iterating until we get it right. When this process works, it means our failures are relatively small in size (most experiments can start small), and when we hit on something that is really working for customers, we double down on it with hopes to turn it into an even bigger success. However, it's not always as clean as that. Inventing is messy, and over time, it's certain that we'll fail at some big bets too."[83]

Failure is an inevitable part of innovation and instrumental to a test-and-learn philosophy. The important thing is to "fail fast"—ban the sacred cows and learn from experience.

Hire the Right People and the Right Mix of People.

With success principles defined, building a culture that supports innovation requires people who either subscribe to the company's values or are willing and able to adopt them.

Specifically, innovation requires participation and involvement from three types of people:

1. **Project leaders** who manage cross-functional teams and drive growth—setting direction, obtaining insights, designing and orchestrating the customer experience.

2. **Smart, creative thinkers and doers** who think outside the box, break paradigms, and generate innovative ideas.

3. **Diverse individuals** who problem-solve from different viewpoints, leading to more insightful, breakthrough innovation.

Though it may be tempting to avoid friction in hiring and staffing decisions, resist this. After all, friction creates sparks, and sparks ignite innovation.

Balancing left-brain and right-brain thinkers leads to a broader range of solutions. "An accountant sitting next to a poet is a really good idea," says Peter Rummell, former chairman of Disney Imagineering.[84] The magic is in the mix.

Steve Jobs expressed it this way: "My model for business is the Beatles. They were four guys who kept each other's negative tendencies in check. They balanced each other, and the total was greater than the sum parts. And that's how I see business. Great things in business are never done by one person; they are done by a team of people."[85]

While employees must have specific expertise, it's best to hire the right people first, knowing they can learn technical skills on the job. (Obviously, there are limits—Disney won't hire an animator who can't draw, for example.) Said another way, hire for attitude, train for skill.

Finally, in setting up teams, be clear about leadership, team goals, roles, and responsibilities. While teams should be self-governing, responding to customer problems as they arise, it's true that if everyone is accountable, no one is accountable.

To avoid diffused responsibility, appoint a team leader accountable for success. When the pressure of everyday business hits—and it will hit—innovation can slip through the cracks unless someone is responsible for its success.

Establish Practices to Support Innovation.

Cultural values are of little importance unless they are embedded in how the company operates. If a company is going to say it's customer-driven, it should be investing in obtaining proprietary customer, marketplace, and technical insights. Similarly, other aspects of upstream marketing—the underlying principles and best practices—need to be operationalized.

Here are a few specific practices to support innovation:

- Establish and broadly communicate the growth strategy to the entire organization

- Develop "idea finding" programs to promote innovation. As Thomas Edison said, "To have good ideas, you need to have a lot of ideas"

- Codify and train employees on upstream marketing principles, approach and a common language

Likewise, to attract and retain the best employees, people-based values need to be baked into human resource procedures, including hiring practices, review criteria, and promotion policies.

The profile companies use strict hiring criteria to ensure they get the right people—those who embody desired cultural traits—on board. This is reflected in the hiring rate of applicants by Apple, Google, Nike, and others, which is less than 1 percent.

Organize for and Commit to Innovation.

A common challenge with innovation is freeing up resources from day-to-day firefighting to focus on the future. This is because innovation beyond the incremental kind requires a different approach.

One way to do this is by creating *dedicated innovation teams*. Under this structure, executive leadership remains at the top, focusing on strategic direction-setting and other corporate initiatives.

Lower levels are then split into core and innovation-focused units. The core organization is functionally oriented, using a traditional hierarchy. The innovation part becomes a flexible network of cross-functional teams from marketing, sales, product development, and R&D.

Innovation teams should be organized like a lean startup—small, entrepreneurial, flexible, and cross-functional.

Amazon refers to them as "Two-Pizza Teams" to describe both the size of the group as well as their entrepreneurial mindset to operate independently and with agility. Bezos believes that no matter how large your company gets, individual teams shouldn't be larger than what two pizzas can feed. A smaller team spends less time administering and more time doing.

Putting innovation decision making in the hands of team members closest to customers reduces corporate layers and speeds up work. The customer, rather than the organizational hierarchy, becomes the judge of how to proceed, which allows team members to work independently.

Whether to *physically separate* innovation from the rest of the organization is hotly debated. As shown here, the profile companies employ separate labs, including dedicated structures, environments, and reward systems.

SAMPLE INNOVATION LABS ACROSS PROFILE COMPANIES

Amazon Lab126 is an inventive San Francisco Bay Area R&D team that designs and engineers high-profile consumer electronic devices, including the Amazon Kindle, Fire, and Echo family of products. The subsidiary is an Amazon lab of innovation, research, and development, and it houses Amazon devices, hardware, software, and operations teams.

Disney Imagineers are a core group of creative professionals who use imagination with engineering (hence "Imagineering") to make dreams reality. Imagineering is the creative force that dreams up, designs, and builds the attractions, cruise ships, real estate developments, and regional entertainment venues worldwide. Building upon the legacy of Walt Disney, Imagineers bring art and science together to turn fantasy into reality and dreams into magic.

Nike's Explore Team Sport Research Lab is a world-class research facility driving performance innovations across Nike. It houses more than forty researchers in scientific disciplines such as biomechanics, physiology, biomedical engineering, mechanical engineering, physics, math, and kinesiology.

Starbucks' Tryer Innovation Center is a 20,000-square-foot space dedicated to innovation. The center is a combination of a makerspace and a Starbucks store where everybody who works at Starbucks can come down and test their ideas. Ideas are brought to life using human-centered design practices and dynamic technical services.

X (formerly known as Google X) is a research center where some of Google's most significant projects happen. These teams work on research that isn't directly tied to a product but encompasses challenging fields like speech processing, machine intelligence, quantum AI, and more.

Deciding whether to establish a separate innovation lab depends on several factors, including the type of innovation planned and available resources. While physical separation can help, it's more about independence from the status quo and access to top executive leadership, recognizing that transformative innovation has unique managerial requirements.

Also, while dedicated labs promote innovation, separate groups alone do not guarantee success. For every thriving corporate innovation center, many more fail, often because they're seen as too disconnected from the core business. Whether innovation occurs inside a company or at another location, corporate and innovation lab strategies must align.

Finally, adequate financial resources need to be in place to support multi-year development efforts. Innovation projects tend to have a longer horizon, and need to be funded and managed as such.

Remember though, just throwing dollars at new ideas won't cut it. Innovation doesn't come from giving people incentives. It comes from creating environments where their ideas collide and connect. Steve Jobs said, "Innovation has nothing to do with how many R&D dollars you have. When Apple came up with the Mac, IBM was spending at least 100 times more on R&D. It's not about money. It's about the people you have, how you're led, and how much you get it."[86]

Aim 'em, don't tame 'em represents the paradox of innovation culture and the natural tension that exists within social organizations. Companies need to embrace strategy and process with an innovative mindset and a culture that is less linear.

To unlock growth, the right principles, practices, and culture all need to integrate into a common upstream marketing approach. Exactly how to do this is described next.

QUESTIONS TO CONSIDER

1. Does the leadership team understand the paradoxical nature of innovation culture and the need to aim 'em, but not tame 'em in driving
   growth?

2. Are the values that support innovation embedded into the organization, and if not, what needs to change?

3. Does the organization have the right practices and structure to facilitate innovation?

NOW APPLY IT:

Integrate and Execute

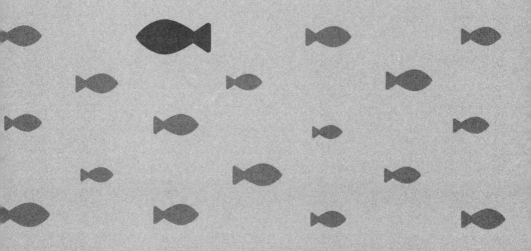

INTEGRATE AND EXECUTE

IN THE PRIOR THREE PARTS, insight, identity, and innovation were presented in isolation, for independent study. In reality, the principles need to be working together all the time.

Here is a recap of six best practices presented in the prior six chapters, with a final wraparound concept—the role of integration and execution—to be discussed next.

1. Maniacally focus on the end customer. Put customers first and look at the business through their eyes.

2. Define a core purpose, then use it to broadly define the playing field and individual demand spaces (i.e., To whom? For what?).

3. Develop winning value propositions at the company, division, and product levels.

4. Elevate brand building to the highest levels of the company. Make the brand a boardroom topic.

5. Deliver a consistent stream of innovative products and services, supported by a flexible, test-and-learn approach.

6. Aim 'em, don't tame 'em to instill a culture that rewards growth, creativity, and risk taking.

In this final part, we integrate the principles and practices into a seven-step upstream marketing approach. Working the steps and guided by the principles and practices, we show you how to implement and practice upstream marketing.

CHAPTER 8

UPSTREAM MARKETING 7-STEP APPROACH

"If there is any lesson I've learned it's that lightning bolts don't hit very often. It is a process and if you don't understand that and if you sit around and wait for the lightning bolt, you're not going to be very productive."

—Peter Rummell, *former chairman of Disney's Imagineers*

"Art resides in the quality of doing, process is not magic."

—Charles Eames, *American designer*

"Plans are only good intentions unless they immediately degenerate into hard work."

—Peter F. Drucker, *author,* The Practice of Management

AT A DINNER WITH A few luxury automotive buyers, held at a top restaurant in Orange County, our consulting team wanted to understand what motivated purchasers of luxury automotive brands.

After some time, one of the dinner attendees felt the need to set us straight with his views: "I'm a jeans and T-shirt guy. I don't wear an expensive watch. I don't live a luxury lifestyle. I just like driving a great car."

Weeks later, we prepared a proprietary customer demand framework, drawing on this and other research inputs, which informed the upstream marketing strategy for launching the client's new luxury automotive brand. The project also resulted in skills transference—the principles, practices, and processes we used are now embedded in the client's organization.

Upstream marketing doesn't just happen. It has to be engineered. Top strategists invest in a systematic approach that leads to profitable business growth. They undertake similar steps to identify strategic opportunity areas, build value propositions, and create strong brands, supported by cultural and organizational enablers.

At the same time, *exactly how* each company approaches upstream marketing varies. Different actions are needed when creating a theme park attraction, developing software, establishing a new sales channel, or targeting a new customer segment.

Industry structure, investment horizons, technical application, time to market, and internal resources affect how each company operates. While the principles hold, they need to be adapted to the situation.

ACTIVATING UPSTREAM MARKETING

Our firm, EquiBrand Consulting, helps companies improve their business performance through a principle- and process-based approach to upstream marketing, integrating with downstream implementation.

Most clients we work with have pieces and parts of upstream marketing—glimmers of insight, identity, and innovation—but lack the integrated whole. Company leaders go from one meeting to the next, one planning cycle to the next, and never bring the pieces together.

To assist them, we use a proven seven-step approach to jump-start upstream marketing, as shown in figure 8.1 and further detailed in the appendix.

7-Step Upstream Marketing Approach						
Phase 1: Where to Play			Phase 2: How to Win			
Set Strategic Direction	Create the Customer Framework	Select Opportunity Areas	Do the Deep Dive	Conduct Focused Ideation	Optimize Concepts	Finalize, Launch, and Learn

Figure 8.1

This approach is broken down into two phases. Phase one, the first three steps, defines where to play, including direction setting, segmentation, and strategic opportunity selection.

In phase two, the final four steps focus on how to win, using deep dives, ideation, concept development, and launch and learn. What would have to be true is asked throughout, consistent with the create-test-and-learn approach. Companies may have multiple upstream marketing cycles going on at the same time, with the approach modified across a portfolio of opportunities.

In executing upstream marketing, it's best to start with phase one. The first three steps should take roughly ninety days, including quantitative research, to establish the opportunity areas and customer framework fact base. If that's impractical, start with phase two, and rely more on qualitatively based inputs.

Think of phase two, How to Win, as a cycle that repeats. This phase also takes about ninety days, depending upon internal and external factors. Each iteration cycle focuses on a limited set of strategic opportunity areas so they can be appropriately resourced and managed.

For example, one cycle might focus on establishing a new business model, another on developing unique value propositions, and a third on penetrating a new customer segment.

The tight timing for each phase is intentional and recognizes both the Pareto 80-20 principle and Parkinson's law.

Purposely reduce the time available and focus on on achieving 80 percent of the value with only 20 percent of the time and effort. With less time, make decisions with partial information. Strive to be "roughly right." After all, many upstream decisions can be reversed. Favor speed and agility over precision and completion. In other words, focus on progress instead of perfection.

To learn, consider an upstream marketing pilot, and then refine the process later. Piloting can offer tangible results while demonstrating the principles, framing questions, and process steps.

As the process unfolds, you may find some things require more attention: The Level 3 customer framework may need to be hypothesized first, then quantified later. Similarly, brand strategy concepts can be drafted now and refined over time.

EQUIBRAND CLIENT CASE

Here's an EquiBrand end-to-end case to show how the seven steps integrate and unfold in practice. Certain facts have been changed to protect confidentiality but the process steps are real.

Our client was considering launching a new luxury automotive brand and hired us to assist with developing the launch strategy and action plan. They wanted to understand, *if* the parent company were to launch a new luxury automotive brand or sub-brand, *how* should it do so to maximize sales and business success?

As background, auto manufacturers do a ton of research, breaking down the market by vehicle type—four-door, midsize luxury, SUV—then further, by benefits the drivers seek—performance versus a comfortable ride or the prestige of a luxury brand.

The problem? The same auto companies subscribe to the same industry reports, yielding the same information. It's not proprietary insight, and it's not enough.

Our client sought a decidedly different view and wanted to

create a consumer demand framework that went beyond the *what*s and *how*s to obtain deep, proprietary insight into the *why*s. Why do individual luxury buyers behave a certain way, based on underlying attitudes and needs?

The project approach involved two phases, each taking roughly ninety days. Phase one focused on strategic direction setting, segmenting the market, and identifying opportunities.

Phase two addressed how to win—defining the value proposition, positioning, strategy, and plan. Here is an overview of each step, including select details—sample interview guides, meeting agendas, and templates—to use in your own organization.

Step 1: Set Strategic Direction.

Any upstream project should be launched with two goals in mind. First, set the project up for success through project planning, and second, establish strategic direction.

PERFORM PROJECT PLANNING TASKS

The first planning task is confirming team roles and clearing project calendars. Four potential team member roles include:

- The team leader who oversees the project and is accountable for its success

- Cross-functional team members to provide specialized expertise

- Executive sponsors, from the C-suite or other areas, to steer the project

- Outside partners like consultants, agencies, and others, to help

Another early planning task is to document additional, related, or redundant activities going on within the organization in parallel. Put these initiatives on a "stop doing" list or combine them with other efforts. This helps free up resources to fund upstream marketing in a more meaningful way.

Also, publish a master project calendar with clear timelines so team members—especially executives—can track progress. "Where'd that come from?" is not a question you want to hear when presenting final recommendations. Upstream marketing involves real-time decision making, and findings build cumulatively, so consistent participation is required.

HOLD PROJECT KICKOFF AND CONFIRM OBJECTIVES

Next, hold a kickoff meeting, lasting from a couple of hours to a full day. The kickoff should confirm project objectives and review upstream marketing principles and processes.

Use the time to share customer insights, hypothesized opportunity areas, and potential solutions. A great probing question: "What do you know about your important customers that your competitors don't know?" Answer this question to inform the situation and identify learning gaps.

CONDUCT A THREE C'S ANALYSIS

Coming out of the kickoff, immerse yourself in the situation. Undertake a three C's analysis—for company, customers, and competitors—to organize relevant facts. Here are details about each component:

Company analysis looks internally to understand the current state of the business and brand, across growth strategies and plans, technical capabilities, brand strength, and product assets.

Customer analysis recaps what you know, think you know, and don't know about the buyer and buying process. Use existing research to inform hypotheses and validate them during Step 2 customer interviews.

- Who are our customers and prospects? How do they segment attitudinally, behaviorally, and demographically?

- What's important to them? Construct a benefit hierarchy to organize product attributes and benefits viewed through the customers' eyes.

- How do they buy? Map the entire decision journey—before, during, and after purchase. Ultimately, you'll want to align brand touchpoints with the customer journey, so begin mapping this early.

Also, spend time analyzing relevant market trends and new technologies, now and in the future. These will help in developing solutions in later steps.

Competitor analysis informs ways to differentiate. You could spend months on this. Do it instead within a week or two. Breakthrough innovation rarely comes from analyzing competitors. Still, there's value in setting a baseline across competitive product offerings, brand positionings, and strategic intent.

CONDUCT INTERNAL INTERVIEWS

Armed with this fact base, conduct internal, cross-functional interviews to fill learning gaps and inform hypotheses development. Here is a high-level sample interview topic guide.

SAMPLE INTERNAL INTERVIEW GUIDE

Objective: To gain perspective on issues, hypotheses, challenges, and opportunities in driving brand and business growth.

Note: The interview should last thirty to forty-five minutes, and only aggregate responses will be reported (to ensure confidentiality).

1. Describe your role, responsibilities, and background (as relevant).

2. What are the leading challenges and opportunities facing the organization today? (What keeps you up at night?)

3. Consider the current state versus future state (i.e., SWOT analysis):

   - What are internal strengths (S) and weaknesses (W)?

   - What are external opportunities (O) and threats (T), including market and technology trends?

4. Who are your customers, what's important to them, and how do they buy? How do they naturally segment based on attitudes, needs, and behaviors?

5. Describe the current value proposition. What benefits do you offer today? What benefits might you provide in the future?

6. In growing the business and brand, what are potential strategic opportunity areas? Probe: new markets, channels, segments, products, etc.

7. How would you define "success" for this project? What barriers need to be overcome, internally or externally, to succeed?

8. Is there anything we didn't ask you that you think is crucial as we move forward with this project?

With our auto client, it wasn't until *after* executive interviews that we realized certain market constraints in launching the brand. Due to several factors, the new brand needed to be sold, at least initially, through its *existing* mainstream dealer network, not via a separate luxury channel.

This would be like Toyota launching Lexus (their luxury brand) and physically locating the brands side by side. This constraint raised a few issues: Was this approach even possible? Would consumers consider purchasing a luxury vehicle physically sold next to its mainline brand? Could we design a luxury experience within the existing channel?

These framing questions guided insight-gathering and remaining project steps. Other questions emerged: Did a consumer segment exist that might be attracted to a new channel approach? How should we position the new brand?

Based on Step 1 findings, we created an initial list of hypotheses, including who to target (a younger millennial consumer), new channel concepts, and success conditions under various marketing scenarios.

Step 2: Create the Level 3 Customer Demand Framework.

The goal of Step 2 is to get out of the office, talk to customers, and create a proprietary to-whom, for-what framework. Use exploratory research followed by quantitative research, ideally, to create the framework.

CONDUCT EXPLORATORY RESEARCH

With our client, we created several interview topic guides across auto industry experts, luxury category influencers (both inside and outside automotive), and end customers.

Our exploratory research included professionally moderated interviews with target consumers behind a one-way mirror. We pre-recruited research respondents and had them complete two "homework assignments." First, inventory and photograph brands they owned—*outside of automotive*—that they considered premium or luxury; and second, take pictures of their existing vehicles to be used later.

The research discussion guide started very broad, about luxury in general, and then narrowed to automotive, including specific vehicle makes and models.

Rather than anchoring on product attributes, we focused on uncovering unmet needs, benefits sought, and jobs to be done. Here's the guide.

SAMPLE CUSTOMER EXPLORATORY INTERVIEW GUIDE

1. Topic introduction, housekeeping, and warm-up exercise

2. Luxury category exploration (outside of automotive)

   • Share homework #1 images with the group

      - *What defines luxury for you?*

      - *What do all these products have in common?*

      - *What's required to be considered luxury or premium?*

      - *With luxury, what "job" needs to be done, rationally and emotionally?*

3. Luxury vehicle discussion

   • Share homework #2 images and discuss currently owned household vehicles

   • Explore needs and benefits sought from luxury vehicles (e.g., ladder rational to higher-order emotional and experiential benefits)

   • *What are you seeking from your luxury vehicle? What job does it do for you?*

   • *Why? Why? Why? (as the basis for benefit hierarchy development)*

4. Customer decision journey and brand touchpoints

   • *Think about your most recent vehicle purchase—before, during, and after the purchase (use flipcharts to structure discussion)*

   • *What were you experiencing, thinking, and feeling at each point?*

- *What were the pain and gain points across the process?*

5. Value proposition requirements and alignment

- *What do you seek with a luxury vehicle purchase? Probe elements (product design, styling, performance; the sales process; service experience; other owner experiences—warranty, financing, trade-in; brand image)*

- *If you could create the ideal value elements/planks, what would they be?*

6. Brand exploration (probe luxury brands and imagery)

- Use sorting exercise to understand perceptual differences across brands

- Probe individual brand imagery using projective techniques—describe the typical driver of each vehicle brand. Where do you fit? Why?

- Probe initial positioning and growth idea "trigger statements"

The goal was to immerse ourselves in the luxury category and target consumer. We explored the customer decision journey and benefits sought from their total experience—who, what, where, how, and, most importantly, why?

What constitutes luxury, both within and outside automotive? Why purchase a luxury vehicle when you can easily get from point A to B at a much lower cost? Why buy one brand over another? The insight helped answer "what would have to be true" in launching the new luxury brand within the mainstream channel.

In addition to traditional research, we conducted roundtable dinner discussions for luxury buyers to interact with each other in a more informal setting.

Coming out of the exploratory sessions, we identified several factors that split consumers into different attitudinal groups.

We learned, for example, that for certain buyers, luxury is seen as a lifestyle that extends beyond automotive—to what they wear, where they travel, and how they live. These consumers like to stand out in a crowd, will only purchase certain brands, and desire a luxury experience, including a high-end dealer service experience. They buy Rolex watches and wear designer clothes.

For others, luxury begins and ends with their vehicle—a fancy showroom and luxury amenities are not necessary. Instead, they find them off-putting. If they could, they'd skip the dealership and purchase their new vehicle online and get it delivered directly to their home.

Across the groups, we mapped the end-to-end customer experience—from pre-purchase (before), purchase (during), and post-purchase (after). We also created a hypothesized customer framework and value proposition, encompassing product, dealer experience, sales, service, and other value planks.

VALIDATE THE FRAMEWORK

After hypothesizing the segments, an optional, though recommended, step is to quantify the segmentation. With our client, we created an online, twenty-minute survey, with a sample of over 2,000 consumers.

This sample was intended to replicate the US population of people in the market for a luxury vehicle. Quantification allowed us to validate hypotheses, confirm unmet needs, fill in data gaps, size, and seize strategic opportunities.

The survey asked respondents to rate their agreement to over seventy-five statements, on a five-point scale, as the basis for defining clear segments. Here are three sample questions, informed by exploratory insight:

- "I'm just a jeans and T-shirt kind of person."

- "I own a luxury vehicle, but I don't really consider myself a luxury buyer outside of automotive."

- "Luxury is a lifestyle that extends into other areas of my life—what I wear, where I travel, and where I live."

Through the hypothesized framework and follow-up statistical analysis, five segments were confirmed quantitatively, with attitudes, needs, and behaviors tightly clustered. Here is a high-level summary of the segments that were fully profiled and sized:

- **Luxury vehicle enthusiasts** consider themselves "car people" and do their research before ever stepping into a dealer showroom. When they get there, they value a hassle-free experience over luxury amenities. For them, a car doesn't need to be flashy, as they're not out to impress anyone. Instead, they look for particular benefits—the latest in features and technology, as well as quality craftsmanship and performance.

- **Luxury brand enthusiasts** look for vehicles with innovative technology, safety, comfort, and performance. They feel that what they drive is a reflection of their personality, and as such, are selective about the brand—they have a specific image to maintain. To them, luxury is a lifestyle that extends to many areas—what they wear, where they travel, how they live.

- **Achievement and experience-oriented consumers** feel the car they drive exemplifies their achievements. They have strong preferences in brands and believe "true luxury" brands have a strong history and heritage. They desire a white-glove dealer experience and want to be treated differently than at a non-luxury dealership.

- **Aesthetics-driven consumers** are concerned with how the car looks and what the brand says about them, not how it performs. They aspire to drive something that uniquely reflects their image—something not everyone is driving. A luxury brand is essential, but they don't value features and technology, so a base model will do.

- **Low-involvement consumers** don't need a flashy car and don't care what people think about what they drive. They may buy a vehicle merely because it's on sale and are less focused on vehicle performance, style, and technology/features. They also wish for a quick, no-hassle sales and service process.

SELECT TARGETS

In confirming targets, common criteria include segment size, attractiveness, and brand fit. In prioritizing segments, it's sometimes easier to first decide who *not* to target than who to target. A process of elimination helps narrow the choices.

With our client, for various reasons, we deleted the achievement-oriented, aesthetics-driven, and low-involvement consumers. We labeled these *consumption* rather than *marketing* targets, hoping to attract these consumers without spending against them.

We then narrowed in on two potential marketing targets—luxury vehicle enthusiasts and luxury brand enthusiasts—for additional investigation. After the groups were identified, a typing tool was created to map actual customers into segments and inform subsequent research efforts.

Step 3: Confirm Strategic Opportunity Areas.

The goal of Step 3 is to identify and prioritize strategic opportunity areas (SOAs), including customer demand spaces. This step involves a strategy session or series of them to confirm the current state, prepare where-to-play strategic opportunities, and develop how-to-win concepts. Here is how the strategy session(s) should unfold.

First, answer the question, *where are we now?* This task involves reviewing the three C's analysis and customer management framework, including bringing consumer segments to life.

Prepare and present segment profiles, including verbal descriptions, photos, and videos of your target (if you have them). Who are they, what do they value, what are the jobs to be done? As questions arise, capture them on a flipchart and answer them during the deep dive in Step 4.

Next, begin with the end in sight. Consider the desired future state and potential SOAs to get there. This step is based on strategy rather than creativity. Strategically identify where to focus and save the blue-sky brainstorming for later.

End the strategy session by recapping high-potential SOAs, filling out a one-page summary for each (as shown in Figure 3.8). Title each SOA and add texture around five points: (1) the target description, (2) customer insight, (3) the need/situation, (4) jobs to be done/benefits sought, and (5) opportunity sizing. Don't be overly concerned about the one-page format, but do write them down.

Finally, prioritize the SOAs using management experience and judgment to narrow the list. Consider the impact-effort matrix or conduct a Harvey ball analysis of the strategic, customer, financial, and operational screens.

Determine which ideas to pursue now, and which to discard or hold for later. Ultimately, limit SOAs to only a few, though the exact number depends on available resources.

With our automotive client, we confirmed two SOAs:

1. Strategically position the new brand, including defining the target consumer, key benefits, and reasons to believe.

2. Develop a relevant and distinctive value proposition to launch the luxury brand within the business constraint of two brands, one channel.

With SOAs confirmed, the process shifts to how to win. The four steps of that phase—deep dive, focused ideation, concept optimization, and launch and learn—are described next.

Step 4: Do the Deep Dive.

The goal of the deep dive (sometimes called the discovery phase) is to obtain in-depth insight into the target consumer, marketplace, and technical solutions to address the specified SOAs.

Up to this point, research with consumers is general in nature— across an "average consumer" to obtain insight on the *entire market* and ensure you're not missing something. Going forward, talk to *target consumers* identified through the customer demand framework, with the end goal of aligning with their needs.

There may be multiple targets to learn from, including current and potential brand users. Typically, a sample of ten to twelve consumers per target is a good number to recruit. After that, diminishing returns set in, with only marginal improvements in insight.

The deep dive with our luxury enthusiast target was to understand their attitudes, needs, and behaviors, including the role the dealer and salespeople played in brand choice and the decision journey. The quantitative research, for example, confirmed that roughly one-third of consumers agreed that "If I could, I would prefer to purchase my vehicle entirely online and never talk to a salesperson."

The strategic opportunity: How might we build on this insight to create a new business model or value proposition to address the two brands/one channel issue? What opportunities existed for redefining the dealer experience? What were the target consumers' unmet needs or jobs to be done?

In addition to consumer research, we designed a separate workstream to understand marketplace forces and factors, including alternative retail formats. This initial strawman draft output provided context for considering alternative retail concepts, as described in figure 8.2.

	Alternative Channel Strategies Probed			
Concept	Separate Channel	Showroom Within a Showroom	Showcase Store	Online Only
Description	Totally separate locations	Separate brands, with a single entrance and unique signage, flooring, lighting	Smaller showcase store, limited selection	Fits with consumer needs (1/3 prefer to avoid dealer entirely)
Example	• Gap vs. Banana Republic • Toyota vs. Lexus	• Polo Shop within Macy's • Best Buy/Magnolia	• Tesla • Nike	• Amazon • Other online
Pros	• Shows commitment • Separates from parent brand	• Cross-shop and compare • Creates perceptual brand distance	• Invest in fewer, more strategic locations	• Fits with consumer desire
Cons	• Cost to build volume • Brand image investment	• Links with parent brand • Superficial separation?	• Limited selection • Location must be accessible	• Cost to build • Brand image expectation and investment

Figure 8.2

As part of the deep dive, we explored how to meet sales and service needs in nontraditional ways. Using "how might we" and "what would have to be true," we focused on two issues:

- How might we create a showroom-within-a-showroom concept—two linked brands—through signage, amenities, and other markers?

- How might consumers skip the dealer showroom experience entirely, using digital technology to create an Uber-like experience?

These issues presented areas to explore during focused ideation, as described next.

Step 5: Run a Focused Ideation.

The goal of focused ideation is to generate new business models, products, services, and other concepts to address particular opportunity areas. In other words, to creatively solve customer problems.

Proven exercises, described in chapter 6, are used to diverge, converge, and generate ideas. The ideas, when related to problem statements, result in breakthrough solutions.

With our client, ideation focused on strategic positioning and alternative channel concepts. For the channel discussion, we broke the process down using a *before, during, after* model (or pre-purchase, purchase, and post-purchase) to describe the customer experience through their eyes. Figure 8.3 provides a snapshot of that raw ideation output.

How might we deliver a luxury experience to target consumers?

	Before (Sales)	During (In Store)	After (Service & Ownership)
Opportunity	Align purchase process with how consumers want to buy, leveraging digital technology, unique store formats, etc.	Develop optimal in-store/in-person experience across various retail formats/scenarios	Develop ownership sub-brand with tiered service levels aligning with luxury ownership
Insight	Growth of vehicle buying services, interest in "no haggle pricing," redesigned channel acceptance, etc.	"We missed the boat—thinking customers want to hang in-store. Most would rather not be there."	"The best service experience is no service experience."

Potential Ideas/ Implications	• Online pre-sale
	• Satellite boutique showroom
	• Pricing program
	  - Transparent pricing
	  - Guaranteed pricing
	• Leasing program
		• Showroom within a showroom
		• Dedicated luxury advisor
		• Self-guided test drive
		• Premium sales kit
			• Online car scheduling
			• Valet service, demo vehicles
			• Free maintenance
			• Lifetime warranty
			• Referral program
			• Certified pre-owned vehicle management

Figure 8.3

Toward the end of the session, we had over 100 numbered ideas on a flipchart, which we narrowed to twelve to fifteen core ideas using dot voting and other prioritization methods, described earlier. We then developed these into written concepts and other stimuli for consumer feedback.

Step 6: Perform Concept Optimization.

The goal of Step 6 is to optimize concepts iteratively with target consumers. Prototypes, in the form of concepts, images, and models, are used to elicit feedback and get closer to the answer.

With our auto client, we developed ideas in two broad strategic areas. The first set of concepts focused on positioning the brand. The second focused on the two brands/one channel issue. Here is an example of a positioning concept.

ABC BRAND. AN EVOLUTION TOWARD SMARTER LUXURY.

Most luxury automotive brands were born in the 20th century, so it's no surprise that they share a more traditional view of what luxury entails. And for many owners, it's all about status—an excessive price tag just to claim exclusivity.

ABC Brand was designed to provide an evolved luxury ownership experience for a new century, born from the belief that the fast pace of life today and technological advances have changed what a luxury vehicle can—and should—be.

ABC Brand prioritizes a smarter, progressive approach to luxury—from the way the vehicles look, to the way they drive, to the way they fit into your life.

The ownership experience has been completely redesigned to maximize your investment, respect your time, and ensure you enjoy all that your vehicle offers. Every ABC vehicle comes with the industry-leading warranty, including free routine maintenance for two years. When it's time for maintenance, a valet will bring a loaner to your door, take your car in for service, and return it to you when it's done.

ABC. An Evolution Toward Smarter Luxury.

Here are a couple of sample concepts used to assess the appeal of alternative sales channel and service concepts.

AT-HOME VEHICLE DEMONSTRATION

A sales representative will bring your vehicle of choice to you for a test drive at the time and location of your choosing, so there's no need to visit a dealership to experience it before buying.

VALET SERVICE

When it's time for service, contact your dealer, and a representative will come to you, pick up your vehicle, deliver a courtesy loaner vehicle, and return yours when it's ready.

Through our concept optimization research (CORE) process, we exposed these concepts and other stimuli to test for appeal, distinctiveness, and credibility. Ideas were shown one by one, then compared against the others.

Throughout the process, we worked with the client in real time to review and revise concepts. This included formal debriefs between consumer research sessions to change stimuli, with concepts added, deleted, and combined iteratively.

With fewer concepts, more time was spent in later research sessions probing details and support points. The result was a set of fully optimized concepts, further tested through quantitative research.

Step 7: Finalize, Launch, and Learn.

Upstream marketing is predicated on the notion of being "roughly right" instead of "precisely wrong" and also on Pareto's 80-20 rule combined with Parkinson's law. This same efficiency/effectiveness bias applies to the final steps in the approach—developing and finalizing the strategic road map and preparing to launch and learn.

When creating upstream marketing plans and integrating with downstream efforts, ditch the 100-page annual operating plan that ends up in somebody's desk drawer. Instead, move to a rolling plan that is revised and reviewed monthly, using a four-page template to track SOA portfolio progress. The four-pager should include the following details about each SOA:

Page one: Describe the customer demand framework (*to whom* and *for what*), including details on the bull's-eye target.

Page two: On the left-hand side of the page, describe the situation-complication-resolution argument. On the right-hand side, present the concept description and visual cues to bring it to life. Answer the questions: What is the core idea, and its winning proposition?

Page three: For the SOA, describe the overarching objectives, supporting initiatives, and corresponding tactics. Figure 8.4 offers an example.

One-Page Upstream Marketing Plan

Objectives	Strategic Opportunity Areas	Marketing Tactics
Confirm marketing objectives and goals	Identify strategic opportunity areas (SOAs) to drive growth	List the tactics supporting each SOA (5–7 bullet points)
• Best to have only 1–2 objectives	Put SOA initiatives in market-based terms	Include supporting detail—cost, timing, and responsibilities
• Objectives should be SMART (i.e., Specific, Measurable, Aggressive, Realistic, and Time-Specific)	It is best to have 3–4 SOAs to focus on	Each SOA should have tactics and each tactic should link to an SOA

Figure 8.4

Page four: Detail who, what, when, and how much including a clear path that shows how to get from where you are to where you want to be downstream. Assign SOA owners, identify major milestones, and confirm the resources made available.

The four-page format forces focus on the most important strategy and plan aspects. At the same time, don't skimp on the rationale. Deep customer insight, including data from concept experiments, should be available in an appendix if someone wants to double-click on supporting detail.

READY. FIRE. AIM.

The final step involves launch and learn—or learn and launch? While some may argue for *even more learning*, leading with *launch* is intentional. With upstream marketing, the traditional directive—*ready, aim, fire*—is replaced with *ready, fire, aim*. In other words, calibrate with the market, launch, and then recalibrate based on market learning.

By now, you've studied the market, talked to consumers, iterated concepts, and answered what would have to be true. Is in-market success guaranteed? Of course not. Still, it's time to launch. For a couple of reasons.

First, business today happens in a blur. Wait too long, and the market moves on. Overanalyze, and it may be too late.

Second, consumers want early access. "You never get a second chance to make a first impression," was a famous tagline for Head & Shoulders when Tim and Kristin worked on the business. While it's a classic line, it's not that true in business today. Most consumers prefer to get an innovation sooner, provided there's a mechanism in place to give feedback if something goes wrong. Also, most business decisions are reversible, even after launch. So take advantage.

In the case of our automotive client, this involved confirming the value proposition, strategic positioning, brand tracking, and multi-year support plan.

As an update, the client successfully launched the brand, with an award-winning product and positioning, and continues to tweak its go-to-market strategy. Importantly, post-launch, the company is responding to market learning and refining its offering and marketing approach. This is consistent with launch and learn, the final—and ongoing—step in the seven-step approach to upstream marketing.

Would your organization benefit from greater focus on upstream marketing? We know it's a lot to take in: three upstream marketing principles, four strategic framing questions, six best practices, and a scalable 7-step process. The final chapter suggests ways to jump-start upstream marketing, including twenty questions to diagnose its impact.

QUESTIONS TO CONSIDER

1. Does your organization have a structured, integrated approach to upstream marketing?

2. Does the approach recognize and answer the framing questions— where to play, how to win, how might we, and what would have to be true?

3. Is the approach informed by insight, identity, and innovation principles and corresponding best practices?

CHAPTER 9

UPSTREAM MARKETING APPLICATION

"Everyone who's ever taken a shower has had an idea. It's the person who gets out of the shower, dries off, and does something about it who makes a difference."

—**Nolan Bushnell,** *entrepreneur and engineer, Atari and Chuck E. Cheese*

"Everyone has a plan until they get punched in the mouth."

—**Mike Tyson,** *boxer*

"Plans are worthless, but planning is everything."

—**Dwight D. Eisenhower,** *34th US President*

IN WRITING *UPSTREAM MARKETING*, EQUIBRAND team members have engaged with hundreds of executives across dozens of categories and industries.

Occasionally, we are asked: "I see how these principles apply to (insert other industry), but will they apply to (insert my industry)?" Potential clients say their customers make purchase decisions solely on price, explain how external factors affect their ability to compete, or declare their industry truly commoditized.

Our answer? Yes, each situation is unique, and yes, upstream marketing still applies. The only common thread across our existing clients is that they are different.

Categories we've applied upstream marketing to include consumer products and services, financial services, health care, industrial products, medical devices, technology, and many others. Some companies are well established. Others are in startup mode. Across industries, there is a range of short and long product development cycles.

In some cases, it's relatively easy to launch prototypes or minimum viable products (MVPs). In others, the cost of developing a physical prototype is prohibitive, with substantial investment required in materials, machinery, and operations.

Here are a few examples of how upstream marketing varies by industry, drawing from our client experiences.

Software development is unique in that new product concepts can often be mocked-up on a computer screen, with the backend replicated to demonstrate functionality.

In these cases, it's straightforward to develop prototypes, beta products, and MVPs to obtain feedback. Prototypes can be iterated until the product is right, before and even after launch.

Apparel companies think in terms of seasons, and therefore continuously look for innovation within a short time frame. For them, trend research—in fabric, design, and color—is a key to business success.

Historically, there were two fashion seasons: spring/summer and fall/winter. Now, certain brands release fifty-two "micro-seasons" annually, which requires rapid-fire concept iteration.

By contrast, automotive companies have long product development cycles. They need to forecast today what the market might look like at launch five or so years from now. What's the future impact of new technologies, demographic shifts, and forecasted fuel prices? They invest in answering these questions through modeling and prototypes to gain market feedback.

Medical device companies have extended development timelines, where the route from an initial idea to a finished, market-ready product can take a half dozen years or more. Getting a medical device approved by the Food and Drug Administration (FDA) places stringent requirements on manufacturers. Specific medical devices—like heart valves and defibrillators—require testing the implants with pigs and sheep before first-in-human studies. A minimum viable product is not an option.

Professional service firms can often test new service enhancements in a pilot setting before a full-scale rollout. In these and other cases, innovation cost and time to market can be very short.

On the other hand, financial services, utility, and health-care companies are often highly regulated, which introduces a host of issues in obtaining market feedback on new concepts.

Below are some real-world upstream marketing cases. While each case is distinct from the others in scope, industry focus, and issue addressed, they all demonstrate the power of insight, identity, and innovation.

Also, company names and case facts have been omitted to protect client confidentiality.

UPSTREAM MARKETING CASE EXAMPLES

Determining Growth Opportunity Areas

CHALLENGE

The leading weekly magazine for celebrity and human-interest stories was under attack from new, lower-priced competitors and a shift toward digital media. The company sought an innovation strategy, process, and specific growth ideas to focus and grow its business.

SOLUTION

Our team worked with the client team in real time to create and pilot upstream marketing. The approach included assessing the current situation, developing an innovation strategy and plan, and working through process steps.

During the internal assessment, we found the brand did not lack for new growth ideas—in fact, the opposite was true. While the company had a strong brand, it had not solidified its value proposition or positioning. With no guardrails to guide innovation, there were almost *too many* brand extension ideas, which risked diluting the brand's equity.

Focusing innovation required developing a relevant and distinctive value proposition framework, then using it to screen ideas. The company's value proposition included these unique brand benefits:

- A cultural source of celebrity and real-life people stories and information

- Journalistic integrity, compared with lower-priced tabloids that ran pure celebrity gossip with less-than-credible headlines

- Entertainment access and exclusive interviews, preferred by celebrity publicists over other titles

Each of these elements was considered in solidifying the brand's value proposition, then used to screen concepts using a Harvey ball analysis.

RESULT

The solidified value proposition and positioning were used to prioritize strategic opportunity areas (to whom and for what) and related innovation concepts (how to win). This screening resulted in fewer, stronger growth concepts. Over time, new initiatives were launched and the company's positioning as a cultural force solidified, allowing it to maintain its leadership and premium pricing, in both online and traditional print environments.

Growing Through Improved Marketing

CHALLENGE

Led by a Stanford-educated plastic surgeon and classically-trained Stanford MBA brand marketer, a leading medical spa was looking to update its brand identity and establish an upstream marketing strategy and plan to fuel growth.

SOLUTION

We used in-depth exploratory research to understand patient attitudes, needs, and behaviors. Projective techniques, including "letters to my body," helped uncover both rational and emotional drivers.

We mapped the consumer decision journey across touchpoints, including pre-purchase, purchase, and post-purchase elements. Then we used concept iteration to confirm the positioning. A digital marketing strategy and plan was developed, drawing on consumer research, keyword research, and marketing analytics.

RESULT

Consumer brand touchpoints—across collateral, website, email, signage, and in-store materials—were redesigned and brought to life through client testimonials and original photography.

A new website was launched, resulting in a doubling of website traffic and a 50 percent reduction in cost per lead, stemming from improved search engine optimization and pay-per-click campaign planning.

The brand continues to expand locations and grow through a consumer-directed, upstream marketing approach.

Positioning a New Product

CHALLENGE

An established medical device company developed a new-to-the-world heart valve that required changes to how cardiac surgeons performed procedures.

While the treatment provided an attractive alternative to conventional approaches, it was challenging to perform and required new surgical training.

The product and therapy needed an effective launch positioning, including defining the target population, framing the category, and confirming benefits and reasons to believe.

SOLUTION

Project steps included assessing the situation, segmenting physicians, and iterating strategic concepts. Exploratory research identified a physician target who, while interested in the new therapy, also needed reassurance, given the new, unproven treatment. A key question needed to be answered first: How should this new therapy be positioned relative to other existing heart valve therapies?

Through concept optimization, we explored alternative ways to frame the new category, recognizing that customers try to "place" a product in an existing category for context.

This framing revealed similarities and differences compared to existing and emerging offerings. Referencing conventional and emerging heart valve therapies provided a "best of both worlds" sense of comfort—that the heart valve was built on a proven platform.

These ideas were included in the product and category launch positioning, as well as visual and messaging concepts.

RESULT

After the trial results, the product was successfully launched in both Europe and the United States. The launch solidified the parent company as the industry leader, providing new therapies and training for cardiac surgeons to extend their capabilities into new medical procedures.

Developing a Strategy for a New Offering

CHALLENGE

The leading semiconductor chip maker and its business partners were looking to launch an integrated solution in the emerging Internet of Things (IoT) market space.

The issue? Market success required a commitment to "the common good." As a group, though, they lacked a shared vision and strategy, and any single company could not create the IoT future alone.

SOLUTION

Developing the solution required working across partner companies (computer processing, hardware, software, networks, and services) as each company played a role in IoT integration. Upstream marketing provided the framework and structure to get consensus and create real-time deliverables through a collaborative, facilitated workshop approach.

Prior to the strategy sessions, we interviewed partner companies and conducted desk research to understand potential gain and pain points.

We synthesized the inputs into a situation assessment and strawman deliverables across demand framework, business model, and positioning perspectives.

We used expert facilitation to establish an aspirational future state and draft an upstream marketing strategy and action items to kick off integrated planning.

RESULT

The collaborative approach established critical relationships and demonstrated the group's potential in working together. The partner companies jointly developed an initial upstream marketing strategy and plan, including prioritized action items, responsibilities, and timing.

Working backward, the group achieved a shared commitment to marketing new IoT products based on group identification and resolution of key marketing issues in moving toward launch.

Extending a Brand to a New Category

CHALLENGE

A leading insurance company wanted to extend its brand beyond traditional insurance offerings (auto, home, and life) to encompass a broader set of financial services, including retirement planning, investment management, and trust services.

Given the company's insurance roots, its brand image anchored on risk management and protection—benefits incongruent with growth investing. Along with a name change—dropping "insurance" from the moniker—the company sought to refine its business proposition and solidify its position in a new category.

SOLUTION

We conducted exploratory research to understand customers' financial security needs and brand perceptions compared to insurance.

Concept statements (initially "unbranded") enabled us to probe customers' financial needs. Once we understood basic needs, we revised concepts to include the client brand name to assess its impact. Did adding the brand name improve or detract from concept appeal? How then should the company position the brand and its expanded role?

Research with existing insurance customers confirmed that many viewed financial services as intimidating and only for wealthy people.

Based on this insight, we created financial-focused concepts to probe deeper. One concept anchored on customers' current financial situations and putting them in control ("No matter where you're starting from, you can obtain financial security.") Another touted a tangible financial plan.

Both areas were worked into the recommended value proposition, positioning, and messaging. Next, we used cross-functional workshops to prepare go-to-market strategies and new communication materials.

RESULT

Adopting the expanded value proposition and promise helped solidify the company's positioning as offering financial security, including a full suite of services.

The project expanded brand associations to improve target customer relevance. The company made changes in company operations, agent training and licensing, and marketing communication materials to support its new positioning.

UPSTREAM MARKETING'S IMPACT

Over the years, we've helped a wide array of clients unlock growth through upstream marketing. Sometimes, a particular issue needs to be addressed—innovation has stalled, growth is suffering, or the organization lacks strategic direction.

In other cases, there is a general desire to grow, with a need for more significant structure and discipline.

Some of our clients have fully embraced upstream marketing, while others are just getting started.

Not surprisingly, the best companies are often the most self-critical. They continually monitor their market position, push themselves to obtain a new future state, and embrace upstream marketing to get there.

Regardless of the starting point, upstream marketing can always be improved. Here are twenty questions—grouped into insight, identity, innovation and integration—to consider for your own organization.

Principle 1: Insight

1. HOW DO YOU DEFINE THE BUSINESS IN WHICH YOU COMPETE?

What is your organization's core purpose? *Why* do you do what you do? Do you define the category based on the needs of your customers or the products you sell? Looking at the business through the eyes of the customer results in more expansive thinking and can help you redefine the playing field.

After defining your market space, think broadly about strategic opportunity areas. *To whom* should you focus and *for what* set of needs? You can use any number of market-based tools and techniques to think about and uncover potential growth areas.

2. WHAT DO YOU KNOW ABOUT YOUR IMPORTANT CUSTOMERS THAT YOUR COMPETITORS DON'T KNOW?

If you don't know who your most valuable customers are or cannot list at least three key insights, that's a problem. Customer obsession and maniacal focus are vital to upstream marketing—it is *the mechanism* for driving growth. So, immerse yourself in the customer experience and look at the business through their eyes.

If you could ask customers or prospects ten questions about their needs and your brand, what would you ask? List the issues, get out of the office, and talk to potential buyers. Alternatively, hire an outside firm to do the legwork. The important thing? Just do it. The insight will prove invaluable.

3. ARE YOU INVESTING IN PROPRIETARY INSIGHTS TO UNLOCK GROWTH?

Don't be fooled by those who cast aside customer research as unimportant. We hear all the time about the flaws of market research—no consumer ever asked for such-and-such invention. People who wanted a faster horse couldn't contemplate the Ford Model T. Researchers in libraries never thought to ask for the Internet. Couch potatoes never envisioned Netflix, with instant access to its array of video content.

However, consumers have always had specific needs—safer and faster transportation, access to organized information, more and better entertainment.

Use whatever terms you like—customer wants, needs, demand spaces, benefits sought, jobs to be done, gain points, pain points, friction points. The key is to ask the right questions and combine this with marketplace and technical insight to solve problems. To win, you need maniacal focus on the customer, because that's where the insights lie.

4. DO YOU HAVE A CUSTOMER DEMAND FRAMEWORK, AND HOW ARE YOU SEGMENTING OPPORTUNITIES, IF AT ALL?

Not all customers are the same, so prioritize and market to groups with similar preferences. A customer framework helps determine both *to whom* you should target your brand and *for what* particular need state. It's a simple, yet powerful concept.

A useful framework can be as basic as listing customer groups across the top (to whom), and needs, benefits sought, and opportunities down the side (for what).

From there, pursue the identified new market spaces. The framework doesn't have to be elaborate or quantified, but it should reflect customer insight and signal potential growth areas.

5. IS THERE A MECHANISM IN PLACE TO REGULARLY INFUSE CUSTOMER, MARKETPLACE, AND TECHNICAL INSIGHT INTO YOUR GROWTH PLANNING?

Get in the habit of getting out of the office and immersing yourself in the customer experience. Do this informally or through a variety of research methods. Practically, if you're in a category that tracks consumer reviews through Amazon, Yelp, or TripAdvisor, start there. Or monitor social listening platforms that integrate Twitter, Facebook, Instagram, and LinkedIn.

Net Promoter Score is another tool to track performance over time, using a simple question: "On a scale of zero to ten, how likely are you to recommend our business to a friend or colleague?"

While tools are a great start, they need to be followed up with other questions, namely "Why?" for deeper insight. Finally, make sure to integrate customer, marketplace, and technical insight. This clarity trifecta is where uncontested market space opportunities emerge.

Principle 2: Identity

6. DOES YOUR COMPANY HAVE AN EXECUTIVE-LEVEL COMMITMENT TO THE IDENTITY PRINCIPLE IN DRIVING GROWTH?

While many C-level executives embrace the principles of insight and innovation, identity is a squishier concept, with benefits harder to quantify.

Skills required to create brands—creativity, design, and brand strategy—are often missing from the boardroom. As a result, brand identity gets relegated to the "marcom" department, treated as a cost with an unclear return on investment.

Elevating the brand to a boardroom topic is critical, and there are a few ways to do this. First, conduct an internal brand audit to compare existing materials to competitors' and best practice companies.

Next, talk to customers to see how they view your brands—are they relevant and distinctive? Finally, ask senior executives if brand efforts support what they're trying to achieve. If any of these check-ins signal opportunities, consider revisiting brand development.

7. HAVE YOU DEFINED YOUR VALUE PROPOSITION IN TERMS OF THE BENEFITS YOUR BRAND SHOULD STAND FOR AND DELIVER ON?

Many companies create corporate-level statements—mission, vision, and values—but stop there. These statements help define an organization's purpose but do little to drive sales. Ideally, companies would apply the same rigor to value proposition development. After all, value propositions tie to value creation and directly link with sales, profits, and future growth.

In creating new offerings, consider and document the three things that matter—customer needs, value planks, and corporate capabilities. Inventory potential value elements to construct individual value planks and entire value propositions. Brand value is what customers get for what they pay. Take credit for the full set of benefits provided and market them accordingly.

8. HAVE YOU DEFINED YOUR BRAND STRATEGY, INCLUDING ITS POSITIONING, EXPERIENCE, ARCHITECTURE, AND EXTENSION STRATEGY?

A brand is one of the few things a company can own forever, so be intentional and actively manage it. After years of helping clients build strong brands, we've narrowed in on four high-leverage brand strategy concepts: brand positioning, brand-customer experience, brand architecture, and brand extension. Do these four things well, and you'll establish a strong foundation for downstream marketing efforts.

9. ARE YOU PRESENTING A COMPELLING BRAND IDENTITY THAT ALIGNS COMPANY ASPIRATIONS WITH MARKETPLACE REQUIREMENTS?

Take a step back and look at the business through the eyes of your customer. Pull up your company website, examine product packaging, post marketing materials in a conference room. How is the brand displayed? Is there a clear purpose and identity? Do the brands fit well together? Are there too many of them? Is it clear what your company offers, why it exists, and how it reflects the customer's desires?

If not, creative strategies and tactics may be out of sync. Consider the role of brand strategy and how upstream and downstream marketing can align to deliver a clear, compelling identity.

10. ARE YOU GETTING THE WORD OUT AND ALIGNING YOUR BRAND TOUCHPOINTS WITH THE CUSTOMER EXPERIENCE?

It's one thing to have compelling, differentiated value propositions. It's another to make people aware of them. Customers need to be informed before they can purchase. Many companies have robust strategies, strong operations, and well-managed product portfolios, but get no credit in the marketplace.

Increasingly, *how* something is communicated and delivered can be as important as *what's* offered. After creating the offer, define and develop a clear go-to-market strategy and plan.

Make it easy for customers to buy from you. Understand the customer decision journey and then map and align brand touchpoints. Elevate the experience. Are you maximizing the value of your end-to-end customer interactions? Or is your brand a light under a basket?

Principle 3: Innovation

11. DO YOU USE AN ITERATIVE APPROACH TO INNOVATION TO OBTAIN INPUT ON HOW TO WIN AND LESSEN RISK?

Concept optimization is a central tenet of upstream marketing. The key steps—deep dive, ideation, concept optimization, and launch and learn—build on each other. Prototypes, ranging from whiteboard concepts to minimum viable products, are used to assess customer appeal and improvement opportunities.

In other words, conduct experiments to learn. Benefits of concept iteration include both lower costs (by weeding out bad ideas early) and greater in-market success, as continuous user feedback helps shape the final offering. Go broad to go narrow.

12. DOES YOUR SCREENING OF INNOVATION CONCEPTS ALLOW FOR SQUISHY, LESS RIGOROUS STANDARDS?

A "prove it" mentality can kill innovation, and new business creation requires a separate focus from the core. Breakthrough innovation is unlikely to occur when applying the same financial thresholds and requirements as those of the existing business.

Testing new business concepts should involve enough latitude for ideas to take shape over time. At least initially, use business judgment and subjective screening, with objective measures used closer to launch.

Ask and answer the question, "What would have to be true?" Use a Harvey ball analysis across strategic, customer, financial, and operational screens. As you iterate concepts, certainty about project success or failure becomes clearer. Closer to launch, quantitative surveys can help project in-market performance.

13. DO YOU TAKE A PIPELINE AND PORTFOLIO APPROACH TO MANAGE GROWTH?

Establishing growth objectives and new product roles is a first step in creating an innovation portfolio and pipeline. Consider a diagnostic audit to help set your financial and strategic goals:

- What percent of sales and profits come from offerings that did not exist one, three, or five years ago?

- Are there coverage gaps in product or market segments that might provide growth?

- What are lessons learned from prior innovation hits and misses?

There's no "right" answer. Still, if you're not considering these questions, or if you see peaks and valleys in sales, it may signal improvement opportunities. Your pipeline and portfolio should be strategically managed to ensure a steady stream of products, representing a mix of incremental, substantial, and transformational innovation.

14. DOES YOUR ORGANIZATION SUPPORT THE AIM 'EM, DON'T TAME 'EM INNOVATION PARADOX?

Annual offsite meeting? Check. Bean bag chairs? Check. Dry-erase whiteboard? Check. Ping-pong or foosball table? Check.

Wouldn't it be great if innovation were as easy as replicating startup stereotypes to guarantee success? Unfortunately, innovation is misunderstood and highly complex. Everyone wants innovation, but few know how to achieve it.

Innovation doesn't just happen. It has to be engineered and requires balancing many factors. Aim 'em, don't tame 'em recognizes the paradoxical nature of innovation and the fun and less-fun corporate values needed to fuel it. The lines between these points are fine, and managing them can mean the difference between success and failure.

15. HAVE YOU PLANNED YOUR CULTURE TO PROMOTE INNOVATION AND GROWTH?

Every organization has a culture, but not every organization has a *planned* culture. It's important to be intentional about culture. Otherwise, one may emerge on its own, and it may not be the one you want.

A review of best cultural and organization practices indicates a common set of cultural values these innovators share. They are: focus and obsess about the customer; employ a growth mindset; think big (but start small and fail fast); ensure the best ideas win; and recognize productive failures. Understand and invest in these cultural traits to set yourself up for success.

Now Apply It: Integrate and Execute

16. DO YOU HAVE A CONFIRMED LIST OF STRATEGIC OPPORTUNITY AREAS TO FOCUS YOUR ORGANIZATION?

Here's a simple question to assess innovation commitment: Is there a documented list of confirmed growth areas within the organization? Without a list, it can be challenging to get attention and funding. Without funding, progress stalls.

Take the time to write down individual SOAs in a clear, consistent format and then collate them into a master list that fills the financial growth gap. Verbal descriptions make SOAs tangible and easy to evaluate so they can be prioritized across the organization. They also force focus on benefits.

Having a single list helps highlight gaps or potential overlaps in efforts to better align resources. Once SOAs are selected, appoint team leaders who are adequately resourced and accountable for success.

17. ARE YOU MAXIMIZING THE VALUE OF THE ENTIRE ORGANIZATION IN DRIVING GROWTH?

Innovation is a team sport that requires active participation from a diverse set of individuals. There's truth to the proverb, "If you want to go fast, go alone. If you want to go far, go together."

Ideally, teams are cross-functional and diverse, making the whole greater than the sum of the parts. Cross-functional teams result in better, faster, and cheaper solutions:

- Ideas are triangulated and improved, with solutions emerging from multiple perspectives.

- Speed to market increases as a natural by-product of dedicated, co-located teams.

- Bad ideas are dropped earlier, concentrating resources on higher-potential areas.

At the same time, individual leadership and accountability are necessary. Appoint one person to make critical decisions, so innovation doesn't slip through the cracks when day-to-day firefighting pressures arise.

18. WHEN WAS THE LAST TIME YOUR ORGANIZATION DEVELOPED AND TRADEMARKED A NEW PRODUCT OR SERVICE?

This question is a bit tricky. On the one hand, if your organization hasn't trademarked a new offering lately, it may be a sign you're missing out on organic growth. On the other hand, it is possible to over-brand. Ask yourself, what is the fewest number of brands needed to support the business objectives?

Many organizations suffer from a chaotic brand architecture with too many competing brands and products. If you are not adequately managing and investing in your brands, they can become empty vessels with no meaning, which contributes to confusion. The brand architecture becomes a mess and needs to be cleaned up.

19. IS YOUR ORGANIZATION SILOED IN ITS APPROACH TO GROWTH?

Organizational silos inhibit communication, innovation and growth, which is why many large corporations look to startups for innovation best practices.

Emerging companies tend to have flatter organizations and stay closer to customers, so information flows more freely. Regardless of company size, there are a few ways to overcome silos and operate more nimbly.

First, establish a common purpose and guiding principles so

employees know what's expected of them. Next, create a well-defined upstream marketing process that breaks down silos and streamlines communication. Processes, by their nature, cut across organizations.

Finally, invest in the power of the consumer and get comfortable doing things with only partial information. In deciding whether to turn left or right, turn instead to the consumer. The marketplace should serve as the ultimate tiebreaker when issues surface, and they definitely will.

Jeff Bezos frequently leaves one seat empty at the conference table where Amazon meetings take place to signify the most important person in the room—the customer.[87] The more customer-driven an organization is, the less siloed it will become.

20. ARE YOU MAXIMIZING THE VALUE OF UPSTREAM MARKETING BY FULLY INTEGRATING INSIGHT, IDENTITY, AND INNOVATION?

You cannot achieve excellence in upstream marketing through a single trait—customer-centricity, a strong brand, or a strategic and cultural commitment to innovation. The critical magnifying effect only occurs when the principles are fully integrated. You cannot pick and choose. You must do them all.

As a Monday morning to-do, review and discuss this set of twenty questions with your team. Ask: Have we established to whom, for what? Have we confirmed how to win? What can be improved?

When looking to improve business performance, it can be hard to know where to focus. Fortunately, there is a proven upstream marketing framework to help. Consider piloting upstream marketing as a team—begin with one or two strategic opportunities. The important thing is to get started. Every organization can benefit from integrating and implementing the upstream marketing principles, processes, tips, and tools found here.

UPSTREAM MARKETING AT EQUIBRAND

At EquiBrand, we're strong believers in the power of upstream marketing and try to practice what we preach.

Each year, we take stock of the prior year's performance, consider client insight, evaluate marketplace trends, and chart new growth strategies and plans for upcoming years. This approach has enabled us to expand our business, develop new service offerings, and reposition our brand over time.

Initial Launch

As background, EquiBrand Consulting was founded in 2000 with the objective of delivering upstream marketing services to our client base. In the early years, we applied the methods described here to establish our identity, positioning, and service offerings.

Starting with the end in sight, we first created a basic website with a pull-down menu of services to frame our thinking. At launch, we offered three core service areas: (1) marketing strategy, (2) brand strategy, and (3) innovation consulting.

We also developed our to-whom, for-what model:

- **To whom:** senior-level executives who recognize the value of investing in marketing and brand strategy services

- **For what:** consulting services across marketing, branding, and innovation, fusing an analytical approach with creativity to grow stronger brands and businesses

We deliberately decided to remain functional, rather than industry, specialists and to serve clients from any sector who find our services of value.

This is not how most management consulting firms operate. For example, McKinsey & Company, Bain & Company, the Boston

Consulting Group, and many smaller firms define their consulting services with a functional/industry cut. They may offer salesforce consulting within pharmaceuticals, financial consulting within telecommunications, marketing for business-to-business clients, and so on.

Still, we decided to keep industry focus open for a few reasons. First, EquiBrand partners grew up in consumer-packaged goods with downstream experience, and many clients found this appealing. Second, as a boutique firm, we were constrained in our capacity to offer specific expertise within a particular industry.

Finally, we wanted to remain flexible and establish a minimum viable product—marketing strategy consulting services—knowing we could adapt, change, and improve over time.

Beyond customer insight and focused services, a key driver of our early success included technical insight obtained by investing in Google AdWords (now just Google Ads) as the primary means of marketing our services.

Though the platform was relatively untested in 2001 (launched just a year earlier), we started placing pay-per-click (PPC) ads to attract clients. We reasoned that digital marketing could "level the playing field" and allow us to compete with much larger firms across the globe. Until then, creating awareness with clients required resource-intensive activities like attending conferences, speaking at events, advertising in trade journals, and face-to-face interaction.

Instead, we focused on becoming technically proficient in digital marketing, including pay-per-click advertising and search engine optimization (SEO).

Through our digital marketing expertise, we were able to get a page-one ranking on Google. One of our first inbound leads came from the Textile, Clothing and Footwear Union of Australia, some 8,000 miles away! Later we'd travel to Adelaide, Australia, to meet with client team members and kick off a project.

Within just a couple years of launch, we had a full pipeline and deepened our expertise. Over time, changes in the marketplace resulted in another shift in approach, as described in figure 9.1.

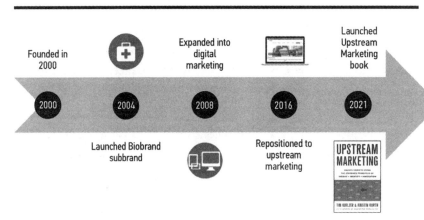

Figure 9.1

Biobrand Creation

In 2004, for example, we reapplied the to-whom, for-what framework to identify new strategic growth opportunity areas.

In the years since launch, we'd gained a number of life-science clients in pharmaceuticals, medical devices, and health care. This in turn attracted similar clients who sought out our specialized knowledge. At the same time, patients and caregivers were taking a more active role in their care, which aligned with our direct-to-consumer expertise. Finally, our marketplace analysis indicated life sciences would continue to grow. Considering these market-based factors, we formalized our commitment to health care, launching a new sub-brand called Biobrand later that year.

Digital Marketing Expansion

A few years later, the Great Recession of 2007–2008 hit, which impacted the market for professional services. Given the choice of hiring outsiders or retaining internal staff, most companies opted for the latter, and spending on consulting evaporated virtually overnight.

Around this same time, traditional management and marketing disciplines were being transformed. The rise of social media, online advertising, digital communication, and the "Amazon effect" significantly impacted how businesses approached marketing. One-to-one marketing—promised for years—became a reality, and money shifted from traditional forms of marketing to digital sources.

We needed to rethink both where to play and how to win. The result? We expanded our service offerings to include digital marketing, drawing on technical insight obtained in marketing our own services.

Competing in digital marketing services required new skill sets across a range of capabilities: digital marketing plan creation, persona development, customer journey mapping, keyword research, off-page and on-page optimization, search engine marketing, and analytics.

Expanding to digital involved changing our downstream marketing as well, including refining our messaging and materials to reflect our new value proposition.

Upstream Marketing Category Creation

Another major strategic shift, beginning around 2016, involved solidifying our position within *upstream marketing* itself. We've had our eye on upstream marketing as a business concept for some time, securing the URL www.upstreammarketing.com back in 2005.

Also, we began to notice competitive shifts within marketing consulting, with ad agencies and marketing companies claiming brand and marketing strategy expertise. This, though, was often a way to sell corporate identity and creative services.

Also, many of these firms were promoting downstream marketing tactics, including social media, as *the* way to grow. This shift prompted at least one frustrated industry practitioner, Tom Doctoroff, to write *Twitter Is Not a Strategy*.[88]

Of course, spring 2020 brought COVID-19 and, along with it, tremendous change. Some industries and companies on the cusp of disruption before COVID-19 did not come back and now look very different on the other side of it. Other organizations were able to pivot to survive.

The need for upstream marketing is even more necessary today as companies seek a way to modify their approach and chart new growth.

Drawing on our intellectual capital and best practice work, we're sharing our upstream marketing tools and frameworks so companies can implement them on their own.

We continue to support upstream marketing through other efforts, including a digital platform for people to exchange ideas and insight. You can visit the site at www.upstreammarketing.com.

Unlock Growth through Upsteam Marketing

After years of helping companies (including our own) grow, we find the critical difference between low-growth and high-growth companies is shaped by their perspective on the role of upstream marketing compared with downstream marketing.

Companies that focus on growing market share on only one playing field wind up over-relying on downstream marketing, which results in lower growth. In comparison, high-growth companies look to redefine the playing field, create uncontested market space, and use insight, identity, and innovation principles to uncover profitable new opportunities.

The strongest brands and businesses are built upstream. The power of upstream marketing is the universal set of principles that work across industries, organizations, and company size. Apply them to your organization to experience the crucial, combined effect in business growth.

And in the words of Dory from Disney's *Finding Nemo,* "Just keep swimming."

QUESTIONS TO CONSIDER

1. Is your leadership team asking and answering the right strategic questions?

2. Does your organization understand and embrace insight, identity, and innovation principles?

3. Would your organization benefit from developing a deeper understanding of upstream marketing through training, workshops, or other methods?

APPENDIX

7-Step Upstream Marketing Framework

Upstream Marketing Principles and Practices		Where to Play?			How to Win?			
		Set Strategic Direction	Create the Customer Framework	Select Opportunity Areas	Do the Deep Dive	Conduct Focused Ideation	Optimize Concepts	Finalize, Launch and, Learn
Insight	Maniacally Focus on the End Customer	✓	✓	✓	✓	✓	✓	✓
Insight	Define Your Purpose – To Whom? For What?	✓	✓	✓				
Identity	Design and Align Value Propositions				✓	✓	✓	✓
Identity	Build and Extend the Brand				✓	✓	✓	✓
Innovation	Create, Test, and Learn (Strategy and Process)					✓	✓	✓
Innovation	Aim 'Em, Don't Tame 'Em (Culture & Organization)							
		How Might We?			What Would Have to Be True?			

ACKNOWLEDGMENTS

UPSTREAM MARKETING IS THE CULMINATION of our life's work, and this book would not have been possible without the contribution of so many. Of course, some of the underlying concepts expressed in Upstream Marketing are not new, but rather draw on proven principles developed by others, including authors, consultants, and colleagues. Rarely do we get a chance to properly thank the people who have influenced and supported our work, and we wanted to do that here.

A number of business books contributed to our thinking, consulting, and writing on upstream marketing:

- David Ogilvy's *Ogilvy on Advertising* shaped our early thinking and careers, including adopting a business approach that balances consumer insights, brilliant creative work, and bottom-line business impact.

- Stephen Covey's *The 7 Habits of Highly Effective People* and *First Things First* advocates a principles-centered approach to leadership, including prioritizing end-in-mind and important-though-not-urgent thinking.

- Al Ries and Jack Trout's *Positioning: The Battle for Your Mind* illustrates the power of frameworks and structured thinking in marketing, specifically, in this case, for positioning development.

- Jim Collin's books *Built to Last* and *Good to Great* draw on case examples and organizing frameworks to demonstrate best practices in business strategy development.

- Ram Charan's *Profitable Growth Is Everyone's Business* coined the term "upstream marketing," which led us to a "eureka moment" in distinguishing it from downstream marketing.

- Philip Kotler's *Marketing Management* and dozens of other titles helped us zero in on the fundamentals, current methods, and future direction of marketing.

- David Aaker's series of books, including *Managing Brand Equity*, *Building Strong Brands*, *Brand Leadership*, and *Brand Portfolio Strategies*, all contributed important concepts and examples of identity development.

- A.G. Lafley and Roger Martin's *Playing to Win* establish a strategy-as-choice approach, including where-to-play, how-to-win, and other cascading questions.

- W. Chan Kim and Renée Mauborgne's *Blue Ocean Strategy* and Alex Osterwalder and Yves Pigneur's *Business Model Generation* demonstrate the power of business strategy canvases in strategy development and tracking.

In addition to these titles, we read dozens of books about Amazon, Apple, Google, Nike, Southwest Airlines, Starbucks, and The Walt Disney Company during our deep dive, as cited in the endnotes.

Real-world experience is where business theory meets practice and is the proving ground for upstream marketing principles and processes. For us, this has occurred throughout our marketing careers, after traveling many miles alongside our clients, testing and learning what works (and what doesn't).

Before EquiBrand, both of us, Tim and Kristin, worked with numerous clients while at various agencies and consulting firms.

These included advertising agencies Tatham, Laird & Kudner, Ogilvy & Mather, BBDO, Magnani, and Hughes Creative. Kristin later formed her own consulting practice, providing strategy and creative services while working with a broader ecosystem of best-of-breed partners.

Tim's work with several management consulting firms—The Cambridge Group, Prophet, and K&A—contributed to insight, identity, and innovation understanding, respectively.

The Cambridge Group influenced perspectives on insight, including the following concepts: benefit hierarchy and ante, driver, and reassurance benefit classification; concept iteration with consumers; customer to-whom/for-what segmentation framework; value proposition; brand relevance and differentiation (including brand asset valuator model developed by Y&R ad agency); brand extension; and related concepts.

Prophet, through David Aaker's work, contributed to identity development, notably how to build strong brands, including brand architecture strategy.

K&A contributed concepts tied to innovation strategy development, including the strategic role of new products and the financial growth gap.

Long story short, EquiBrand Consulting started unexpectedly over 20 years ago, when Tim and Kristin moved West for the second gold rush—chasing the Internet bubble that would burst within a year. Necessity proved to be the mother of invention. Starting with a blank page, we distilled the best thinking from the experiences listed prior into an initial set of upstream marketing principles and corresponding services, which expanded over time.

Our colleagues at EquiBrand Consulting, including Becky Charles, Joel Friedman, Chris Rei, Michelle Sanchez, Jo Thorogood, and Mike Zeinfeld, have contributed extensively to EquiBrand's intellectual property and client work, as well as directly and indirectly to *Upstream Marketing*. We are fortunate to work with such an amazing set of professionals.

We sought out and received feedback on early drafts from three brilliant A-to-Z strategists, Pablo Azar, Stuart Hilger, and Mark Zobel, who significantly enhanced the final product.

We are grateful for the team at Greenleaf Book Group, including Lindsay Bohls, Lindsey Clark, Neil Gonzales, Amanda Hughes, and O'Licia Parker-Smith. Thank you for your creative contributions as well as for keeping us on task and on target.

The biggest thank-you goes to our EquiBrand clients and collaborators over the years. There would be no *Upstream Marketing* without you all, and every client project we work on challenges our thinking and shapes our perspectives.

Then there are the various tribes of close friends and colleagues—from childhood, college, Chicago, and California friends to client team members who impacted this effort. A story told in one setting—dinner with close friends—combined with an experience shared in another—the client backroom of a focus group facility—and business clarity emerged. Looking back, the hundreds of disparate personal and professional experiences throughout this journey don't seem so random after all.

We'd also like to thank our families. For Tim, this includes his parents, Jim and Mary Ellen, as well as his brothers and sisters, too many to list here (not really, but almost). Tim's eleven siblings are Kathy, Jim, Julie, Pete, Tom, Mary, Mike, Jane, Therese, Jenny, and David. Growing up in a family of twelve kids teaches a lot, and many of those lessons contributed to writing this book.

Kristin is grateful to her family—parents Phil and Judy and siblings Kenton and Kara—her biggest fans and first "team" who taught her about group dynamics, communication, and integrity.

Finally, as both work and life partners for over 35 years, we'd like to thank each other and our four children—Kit, Matt, Maddie, and Isaac. Writing this book has been unbelievably challenging, yet equally rewarding, and could only have been achieved through your unconditional patience, love, and support.

NOTES

1. Keating, Steve, "Brazil Still in Love with Iconic Strip," June 13, 2014. See also: https://www.reuters.com/article/us-soccer-world-bra-kit/brazil-still-in-love-with-iconic-strip-idUSKBN0EO29W20140613

2. Charan, Ram, *Profitable Growth is Everyone's Business: 10 Tools You Can Use Monday Morning* (New York: Random House, 2004), page 30.

3. Lafley, A.G., and Roger L. Martin, *Playing to Win: How Strategy Really Works,* 5th ed. (Harvard Business Review Press, 2013).

4. https://hbr.org/2012/09/the-secret-phrase-top-innovato

5. Hall, Stephen, Dan Lovallo, and Reinier Musters, "How to Put Your Money Where Your Strategy Is," *McKinsey Quarterly*, March 2012.

6. Low, Elaine, "Disney Reorganizes Content and Distribution Units to Bolster Streaming Businesses," *Variety*, October 12, 2020. See also: https://variety.com/2020/tv/news/walt-disney-structural-reorganization-media-entertainment-business-1234801683/

7. McKinsey Growth & Innovation Survey; McKinsey & Company analysis. See also: https://www.mckinsey.com/business-functions/strategy-and-corporate-finance/how-we-help-clients/growth-and-innovation

8. Rossman, John, *Think Like Amazon* (New York: McGraw-Hill, 2019); Levy, Steven, "Jeff Bezos Owns the Web in More Ways Than You Think," *Wired*, November 13, 2011. See also: https://www.wired.com/2011/11/ff_bezos/

9. Benett, Andrew, Ann O'Reilly, Cavas Gobhai, *Good for Business: The Rise of the Conscious Corporation*, (New York: Macmillan, 2010). See also: https://books.google.com/books?id=eonvCgAAQBAJ&pg=PA156&lpg=PA156&dq=aim+em+dont+tame+em+cavas+gobhai&source=bl&ots=7jamvVIQd5&sig=ACfU3U1mlr55GiEzT4W3tOKy8TY7dOHX3Q&hl=en&sa=X&ved=2ahUKEwj7tZ6quujpAhWQsZ4KHfPIBPoQ6AEwAHoECAoQAQ#v=onepage&q=aim%20em%20dont%20tame%20em%20cavas%20gobhai&f=false

10. Carson, Biz, "Steve Jobs' Reaction to This Insult Shows Why He Was Such a Great CEO," *Business Insider,* October 22, 2015. See also: https://www.businessinsider.com/steve-jobs-reaction-to-insult-2015-10

11. Poletick, Rachel, "7 Theme Parks That Inspired Disneyland," *Mental Floss,* March 19, 2014. See also: https://www.mentalfloss.com/article/55642/7-theme-parks-inspired-disneyland

12. Gennawey, Sam. "SAMLAND. How Walt Disney Studied and Built Disneyland," MiceChat, June 27, 2012. See also: https://www.micechat.com/224-walt-disney-disneyland/

13. Dauble, Jennifer, "CNBC Exclusive: CNBC's Maria Bartiromo Interviews Google CEO Eric Schmidt, Today on 'Closing Bell with Maria Bartiromo,'" CNBC, April 30, 2008. See also: https://www.cnbc.com/id/24386465

14. Reiss, Christopher, Quora, March 17, 2013. See also: https://www.quora.com/What-are-the-valuable-differences-between-knowledge-wisdom-and-insight-Beyond-their-basic-definitions-what-benefits-do-they-hold/answer/Christopher-Reiss

15. Bezos, Jeff, 2016 letter to shareholders, posted April 17, 2017. See also: https://blog.aboutamazon.com/company-news/2016-letter-to-shareholders

16. Dead Poets Society, "The Universe Is Wider than Our Views of It (Thoreau)." See also: https://www.youtube.com/watch?v=U91Wl2YpkD8

17. Wolf, Gary, "Steve Jobs: The Next Insanely Great Thing," *Wired*, February 1, 1996. See also: https://www.wired.com/1996/02/jobs-2/

18. "Steve Jobs on Product Design," Impact Interview, posted August 25, 2011. See also: https://www.impactinterview.com/2011/08/steve-jobs-on-product-design-2/

19. Berfield, Susan, "It's Schultz vs. Schultz at Starbucks," NBC News, updated August 10, 2009. See also: http://www.nbcnews.com/id/32336151/ns/business-us_business/t/its-schultz-vs-schultz-starbucks/#.Xo87vMhKhPY

20. Bezos, Jeff, 2016 letter to shareholders, posted April 17, 2017. See also: https://blog.aboutamazon.com/company-news/2016-letter-to-shareholders

21. Gennawey, Sam, *Walt and the Promise of Progress City* (Lexington, KY: Theme Park Press, 2014).

22. Goldsby, Michael G. and Rob Mathews, *Entrepreneurship the Disney Way* (New York: Routledge, 2019).

23. Levitt, Theodore, "Marketing Myopia," *Harvard Business Review,* July–August 2004. See also: https://hbr.org/2004/07/marketing-myopia

24. "Apple Presents iPod," October 23, 2001. See also: https://www.apple.com/newsroom/2001/10/23Apple-Presents-iPod/

25. Umoh, Ruth, "Why Jeff Bezos Makes Amazon Execs Read 6-Page Memos at the Start of Each Meeting," CNBC Make It, April 23, 2018, https://www.cnbc.com/2018/04/23/what-jeff-bezos-learned-from-requiring-6-page-memos-at-amazon.html

26. Starbucks mission statement. See: https://www.starbucks.com/about-us/company-information/mission-statement

27. Rusbridger, Alan, "The Future According to Mr. Google," *The Guardian,* April 19, 2013. See also: https://www.theguardian.com/technology/2013/apr/20/eric-schmidt-google-alan-rusbridger

28. Kelly, Gary, "Gary's Greeting: Best in Flight." See also: https://www.southwest.com/assets/pdfs/about-southwest/garys-greeting.pdf

29. Quoted in Jones + Waddell, "That One Time Southwest Airlines Altered the Airline Model," January 24, 2020. See also: https://medium.com/@joneswaddell/that-one-time-southwest-airlines-altered-the-airline-model-7cbb257545e3

30. Southwest purpose statement. See: https://www.southwest.com/html/about-southwest/index.html

31. "Earth's Most Customer-Centric Company," Amazon Jobs website. See also: https://www.amazon.jobs/en-gb/working/working-amazon

32. D'Onfro, Jillian, "17 Quotes that Show How Jeff Bezos Turned Amazon into a $200 Billion Company over 20 Years," *Business Insider,* July 16, 2015. See also: https://www.businessinsider.com/amazon-ceo-jeff-bezos-quotes-2015-7

33. Nike purpose statement. See: https://purpose.nike.com/

34. Willigan, Geraldine E., "High-Performance Marketing: An Interview with Nike's Phil Knight," *Harvard Business Review*, July–August 1992. See also: https://hbr.org/1992/07/high-performance-marketing-an-interview-with-nikes-phil-knight

35. Burrows, Peter, "Back to the Future at Apple," *Bloomberg*, May 25, 1998. See also: https://www.bloomberg.com/news/articles/1998-05-24/back-to-the-future-at-apple

36. Rasmus, Daniel W., "Defining Your Company's Vision," *Fast Company,* February 28, 2012. See also: https://www.fastcompany.com/1821021/defining-your-companys-vision

37. As quoted in the ending credits of the movie *Meet the Robinsons* (2007), https://en.wikiquote.org/wiki/Walt_Disney

38. Sinek, Simon, *Start with Why: How Great Leaders Inspire Everyone to Take Action* (New York: Penguin, 2011), page 41.

39. Yarow, Jay, "This Is the Super Simple Chart Steve Jobs Made to Save Apple from Extinction," *Business Insider,* October 24, 2011. See also: https://www.businessinsider.com/chart-that-saved-apple-2011-10

40. Ansoff, Igor, "Strategies for Diversification," *Harvard Business Review,* Vol. 35, Issue 5, Sep–Oct 1957, pages 113–124. See also: https://en.wikipedia.org/wiki/Ansoff_Matrix

41. Rothaermel, Frank T., and Noorein Inamdar, *The Walt Disney Company (New York: McGraw-Hill Education, 2017); www.disney.com; Atkins, Stuart, "25 Segmentation Variables for Consumer Markets: Phillip Kotler," Atkins Marketing Solutions, December 16, 2011.*

42. Willigan, Geraldine E., "High-Performance Marketing: An Interview with Nike's Phil Knight," *Harvard Business Review*, July–August 1992. See also: https://hbr.org/1992/07/high-performance-marketing-an-interview-with-nikes-phil-knight

43. "Steve Jobs Speaks Out, America's Most Admired Companies 2008," *CNN Money*, last updated March 7, 2008, https://money.cnn.com/galleries/2008/fortune/0803/gallery.jobsqna.fortune/4.html

44. Schultz, Howard, *Business Leadership Masterclass* video series (2019).

45. "Message from Howard Schultz to Partners: Onward with Love," Starbucks Stories & News website, June 4, 2018. See also: https://stories.starbucks.com/stories/2018/message-from-howard-schultz-to-partners-onward-with-love/

46. Wagner, Rodd, "Happy Employees Equal Happy Customers? Well, Yes, But It's Complicated," *Forbes*, February 27, 2017. See also: https://www.forbes.com/sites/roddwagner/2017/02/27/happy-employees-equal-happy-customers-well-yes-but-its-complicated/#2e397a9f7c6e

47. Hollis, R., and B. Sibley, *Snow White and the Seven Dwarfs & the Making of the Classic Film* (New York: Hyperion, 1994).

48. Schultz, Howard, *Pour Your Heart into It: How Starbucks Built a Company One Cup at a Time* (Hachette Books, 1997).

49. Arruda, William, "The Most Damaging Myth About Branding," *Forbes*, September 6, 2016. See also: https://www.forbes.com/sites/williamarruda/2016/09/06/the-most-damaging-myth-about-branding/#64cba3775c4f

50. Richter, Millie, "Southwest Airlines Reveals Our Heart with Bold New Look," Southwest Air Community blog, September 8, 2014. See also: https://community.southwest.com/t5/Blog/Southwest-Airlines-Reveals-Our-Heart-with-Bold-New-Look/ba-p/46028

51. Horovitz, Bruce, "Starbucks CEO Schultz on Digital Innovation," *USA Today*, April 24, 2013. See also: https://www.usatoday.com/story/money/business/2013/04/24/starbucks-howard-schultz-innovators/2047655/

52. Goldsby, Michael G. and Rob Mathews, *Entrepreneurship the Disney Way* (New York: Routledge, 2019), page 76.

53. Markides, Constantinos C., "To Diversify or Not to Diversify," *Harvard Business Review*, November–December 1997. See also: https://hbr.org/1997/11/to-diversify-or-not-to-diversify

54. Zener, Todd, "The Disney Recipe," *Harvard Business Review*, May 28, 2013. See also: https://hbr.org/1997/11/to-diversify-or-not-to-diversify

55. Jones, Bruce, "Leadership Lessons from Walt Disney: Communicating a Vision," Disney Institute Blog, July 24, 2018. See also: https://www.disneyinstitute.com/blog/leadership-lessons-from-walt-disney-communicating-a-vision/

56. Beattie, Andrew, "Walt Disney: How Entertainment Became an Empire," Investopedia, July 26, 2020. See also: https://www.investopedia.com/articles/financial-theory/11/walt-disney-entertainment-to-empire.asp

57. Johnston, Ollie and Frank Thomas, *The Illusion of Life: Disney Animation* (New York: Abbeville Press, 1981).

58. Google website: https://gsuite.google.co.in/intl/en_in/learn-more/creating_a_culture_of_innovation.html; EquiBrand analysis

59. https://www.quora.com/What-is-Amazons-approach-to-product-development-and-product-management

60. Price, Harrison "Buzz," *Walt's Revolution!: By the Numbers* (New York: Ripley Entertainment, 2004).

61. Mathur, Ashish, "Michael Jordan's NBA Contracts." See: https://clutchpoints.com/michael-jordan-nba-contracts

62. Ahuja, Pavni, "Nike Was Never the First Choice of Jordan for Sneaker Deal But Others Refused to Give an Offer." See: https://www.essentiallysports.com/nba-news-chicago-bulls-nike-was-never-the-first-choice-of-michael-jordan-for-sneaker-deal-but-others-refused-to-give-an-offer

63. Google, "Creating a Culture of Innovation: Eight Ideas that Work at Google." See also: https://gsuite.google.co.in/intl/en_in/learn-more/creating_a_culture_of_innovation.html

64. Johnson, Bruce D., "My Favorite Steve Jobs Quotes on Innovation and Creativity, Wired To Grow." See also: http://www.wiredtogrow.com/steve-jobs-on-innovation/

65. Bezos, Jeff, 2016 letter to shareholders.

66. Jacka, Mike, "You've Got to Be Kidding: Disney, Light Bulbs, and the Screwing In of the Same," MiceChat, May 4, 2019. See also: https://www.micechat.com/223225-youve-got-to-be-kidding-disney-light-bulbs-and-the-screwing-in-of-the-same/

67. Schmidt, Eric, and Jonathan Rosenberg, *How Google Works* (New York: Grand Central Publishing, 2014).

68. Schmidt, *How Google Works*, page 20.

69. Pisano, Gary P., "The Hard Truth About Innovative Cultures," *Harvard Business Review,* January 9, 2019. See also: https://www.bizjournals.com/bizjournals/news/2019/01/09/hbr-the-hard-truth-about-innovative-cultures.html

70. "Leadership Principles," Amazon Jobs. See: https://www.amazon.jobs/en-gb/principles

71. Brandt, Richard L., "Birth of a Salesman; Behind the Rise of Jeff Bezos and Amazon," *Wall Street Journal* (online), October 15, 2011.

72. "What Is Nike's Mission?" Nike. See: https://www.nike.com/help/a/nikeinc-mission

73. Nike statement on values and innovation, Life at Nike. See: https://jobs.nike.com/life-at-nike#

74. Bennett, Donnovan, "My Work of Art Is Nike," interview with

Phil Knight, *Sportsnet.* See: https://www.sportsnet.ca/more/
nike-founder-phil-knight-story-culture-behind-sports-apparel-juggernaut/

75. Zorn, Eric, "Without Failure, Jordan Would Be a False Idol," *Chicago Tribune,*
May 19, 1997. See also: https://www.chicagotribune.com/news/ct-xpm-1997-05-
19-9705190096-story.html

76. Southwest's purpose, vision, and values on the Southwest jobs website. See:
https://www.southwest.com/html/about-southwest/careers/culture.html;

77. Byrant, Adam, "Good C.E.O.'s Are Insecure (and Know It)," interview with
Howard Schultz, *The New York Times,* October 9, 2010. See also: https://www.
nytimes.com/2010/10/10/business/10corner.html

78. Starbucks' mission and values on the Starbucks Stories & News website, last
updated December 15, 2015. See: https://stories.starbucks.com/stories/2015/
starbucks-mission-and-values

79. The Walt Disney Company mission. See: https://thewaltdisneycompany.com/
about/

80. "Mickey's Ten Commandments" quoted from Martin Sklar, "Walt Disney
Imagineering, Education vs. Entertainment: Competing for Audiences," AAM
Annual meeting, 1987. See also: https://airandspace.si.edu/rfp/exhibitions/files/
j1-exhibition-guidelines/3/Mickeys%2010%20Commandments.pdf

81. Petro, Greg, "Nike Just Does It—Keeping an Eye on the Customer," *Forbes,*
July 8, 2016. See also: https://www.forbes.com/sites/gregpetro/2016/07/08/
nike-just-does-it-keeping-an-eye-on-the-customer/#33b8f4da56da

82. Schmidt, Eric, "What Does a Networked Future Look Like?" *Yale
Insights*, May 15, 2013. See also: https://insights.som.yale.edu/insights/
what-does-networked-future-look-like

83. Bezos, Jeff, 2014 letter to shareholders. See: https://www.sec.gov/Archives/edgar/
data/1018724/000119312514137753/d702518dex991.htm

84. Greenfield, Rebecca, "How Disney's Imagineers Keep the Magic Ideas Coming,"
Fast Company, May 2, 2014. See: https://www.fastcompany.com/3029906/
how-disneys-imagineers-keep-the-magic-ideas-coming

85. Farber, Dan, "Tim Cook Maintains Steve Jobs' Beatles Business
Model," CNET, June 12, 2013. See also: https://www.cnet.com/news/
tim-cook-maintains-steve-jobs-beatles-business-model/

86. Kirkpatrick, David, "The Second Coming of Apple Through a Magical Fusion of
Man—Steve Jobs—and Company," *Fortune,* November 9, 1998. See also: https://
archive.fortune.com/magazines/fortune/fortune_archive/1998/11/09/250834/
index.htm

87. Anders, George, "Inside Amazon's Idea Machine: How Bezos Decodes
Customers," *Forbes,* April 4, 2012. See also: https://www.forbes.com/sites/
georgeanders/2012/04/04/inside-amazon/#7a45671c6199

88. Doctoroff, Tom, *Twitter Is Not a Strategy: Rediscovering the Art of Brand Marketing*
(New York: St. Martin's Press, 2014).

INDEX

UPSTREAM MARKETING RESOURCES

Visit www.upstreammarketing.com/resources to learn more about the power of upstream marketing, including training videos, practical tips, and downloadable content.

Upstream Marketing Framework

Module 1: An Overview

Principles	Insight	Identity	Innovation
Framing Question	Where to Play?	How to Win?	How Might We?
Best Practices	Module 2	Module 4	Module 6
	Maniacally Focus on the End Customer	Design and Align Value Propositions	Create, Test, and Learn (Strategy & Process)
	Module 3	Module 5	Module 7
	Define Your Purpose— To Whom? For What?	Build and Extend the Brand	Aim 'Em, Don't Tame 'Em (Creativity & Culture)

Process: Integrate and Execute

Framing Question: What Would Have to Be True?

Module 8	Module 9
Upstream Marketing 7-Step Approach	Upstream Marketing Application

ABOUT THE AUTHORS

Tim Koelzer—Tim is the leading authority on and practitioner of upstream marketing and the three underlying principles of insight, identity, and innovation.

As the co-founder and managing partner of EquiBrand Consulting. Tim leads client engagements in helping companies grow strong brands and businesses. In his role, Tim brings broad and deep professional experience to strategic marketing and planning, brand building, and new product development.

Tim works across a spectrum of companies—from global Fortune 500 companies to venture-backed startups, within business-to-business and business-to-consumer settings.

Industries he's worked in include apparel, automotive, consumer products, financial services, food, healthcare, industrial products, insurance, medical devices, technology and others.

His client list reads like a *who's who* of top global brands and businesses. See EquiBrandConsulting.com for details.

Prior to EquiBrand, Tim worked for several other management consulting firms including Prophet, The Cambridge Group, Accenture, and Kuczmarski Innovation, where he directed a range of client engagements. Tim began his career in the advertising industry, in account management at Ogilvy Chicago and media planning with another agency.

Tim received a BA in advertising from Michigan State University and an MBA from the J. L. Kellogg Graduate School of Management at Northwestern University, with concentration in marketing and finance.

Kristin Kurth—Kristin has an accomplished career in both upstream and downstream marketing. Her perspective comes from working across a wide range of industries including consumer and luxury goods, financial services, automotive, healthcare/biotech, publishing, real estate, hospitality, technology, and for an array of non-profits.

Kristin co-founded EquiBrand Consulting, helping clients from startups to Fortune 100 companies strategize, plan, and launch integrated brand-building initiatives. She has developed an extensive ecosystem of marketing and brand-building partners who contribute to EquiBrand engagements as needed.

Kristin began her career in advertising as a media planner on the Procter & Gamble business. She then worked in account management at BBDO and Ogilvy Chicago on packaged goods businesses, spending the majority of her career at Ogilvy, where she was a Senior Partner/Worldwide Management Supervisor in charge of the Wilson Sporting Goods business globally.

Kristin has a BBA from the University of Michigan Ross School of Business and an MBA from the University of Chicago Booth School of Business, with specialization in marketing, finance, and economics.

She is an adjunct professor of marketing in the undergraduate and graduate programs of the School of Economics and Business Administration at St. Mary's College in Moraga, California. Kristin has also guest lectured extensively at top MBA programs, including Stanford Graduate School of Business, Haas Business School at University of California Berkeley, Northwestern's Kellogg School of Management, and the University of Chicago's Booth School of Business.